Time

Served

"If Christ Shall Make You Free, You Shall Be Free Indeed"

Serving more than thirty years of ministry in one of America's most controversial prison systems, Wendy "Ma" Hatcher, recounts her experiences as a State Chaplain at the notorious Parchman Prison Farm in the Mississippi Delta.

In a unique mixture of reality and compassion, Wendy offers a perspective that leaves the reader balancing precariously between sympathetic forgiveness and righteous anger.

Whichever side of the barbed wire fence one falls on after reading her story, one thing is for sure, all eyes are raised upwards, above and beyond the earthly ties that bind, toward the One who sets all captives free.

Time

Served

Chaplain
Wendy Hatcher

CROSSOVER
WWW.CROSSOVERPUBLICATIONS.COM
PUBLICATIONS

CROSSOVER

WWW.CROSSOVERPUBLICATIONS.COM

PUBLICATIONS

Time SERVED

WENDY HATCHER

Copyright © 2016 by Wendy Hatcher

Published by:
Crossover Publications
Houston, Texas 77084
USA
All Rights Reserved

All Scripture quotations, unless otherwise indicated are taken from The KING JAMES VERSION of the Bible.

Library of Congress Control Number: 2016942601

ISBN 978-0-9837496-4-6

Cover concept and design: Matthew Mooney & Randall Mooney
Interior design: Randall Mooney
Cover photos provided by: Wendy Hatcher
Back cover photo: William Powell Photography

Printed in the USA

Dedicated to

To my savior, Jesus Christ, without whom
there would only be a sad story.
To my dear, precious children:
John, my technical whizz and solid rock;
Wendy Leigh, journalist & editor,
for her expertise in these pages;
Glynis, R.N. & attorney,
my own special counselor;
and Bill, sports coach who always comes
when I call, giving sometimes unwanted
but always sensible, practical advice.
To their spouses, Lynn, Doug and Mitzi
so special to me.
And to my brother, Ted,
so far away in England, but so loved.
And to my seven Grandchildren and their
spouses, and my six Great-Grandchildren.

My cup runneth over.

For the hundreds of unnamed people who bring
me joy just thinking about them. I am eternally
grateful. God knows who they are.

Table of Contents

Foreword

Time Served is an accurate account of how a little English lady from humble beginnings became a prison chaplain, endured many personal challenges, and dedicated her life to sharing her heart and love with broken people who needed hope and direction.

I came to know Wendy Hatcher while serving as the Warden of two prisons at which she served as a Chaplain. For over 30 years, I witnessed the positive impact of her ministry. Wendy's friendship and ministry also had a major influence on my life. She convinced me that even those who have committed unspeakable crimes against humanity can change. I have never had a truer teacher.

Her life is a living example of how putting Christ's love in action, being humble and repentant, can bring hope and peace to people in a downward spiral. The key takeaway from Wendy's inspiring book is how prison ministry changes lives, even in this tough and hostile environment. This is evident through her works. It is a must read!

Raymond Roberts
Secretary of Corrections
Kansas Department of Corrections

Fueled with zeal for the Lord, Wendy Hatcher entered the prisons to teach His Word and spread His love. An unlikely background of having come from England as a young women and having reared four children in the rural Mississippi Delta, Wendy first taught in the jails and later as a prison chaplain. She regularly encountered difficulties, both with the angry inmates and with prison bureaucracy. Her unselfish devotion to those imprisoned earned her the name of "Ma" to the many she influenced. This book shows the power of God working through a Christian willing to serve Him in places where many fear to tread, and it reveals lives changed through her courageous efforts.

Laurence Y. Mellen
26 years as District Attorney
11th Circuit District of the State of Mississippi

Chapter One

Time Served

On the drive through Mississippi Delta farmlands, blanketed in late summer with the endless rows of blooming cotton, one could almost feel that all was right with the world. Like the neatly planted cotton seeds of early Spring, which opened slowly with the heat of summer and now stood ready to harvest, my own future was unknowingly unfolding with each mile. The year was 1965, and I was driving toward the notorious Parchman Prison Farm.

Armed only with a Bible, and permission to enter the prison grounds with a group from my church, I had no idea that the next 30 years of my life would be spent offering hope and freedom to those who had neither. As an avid church-goer, I routinely volunteered for the latest committee or ministry. The "social Christianity" which I knew at the time, however, prepared me very little for the reality of a world filled with murderers and thieves.

As our car wove its way through the thousands of acres of cotton, rice and bean fields along the dusty roads toward the prison, we were following what I now know was God's calling on my life. I was free to turn back at any moment, yet destined to travel the path that led into the place of bondage for thousands of captive men and women who were as yet unknown to me.

The Mississippi Delta had become my adopted home after marrying a Southern Gentleman, and moving an ocean away from the fishing village outside London that had been my world. I settled in the town of Cleveland, Mississippi, population 10,000, most of whom I knew socially, as the wife of a prominent attorney. Now, some 13 years and four children later, I was entering what would become a full-time ministry as a State Chaplain in one of the most controversial prisons in America.

Established in 1904 by then Governor James K. "White Chief" Vardaman, Parchman Penitentiary was set up to be a profitable prison labor farm. It covered more than 20,000 acres, spanning 46 square miles, and initially housing a sawmill, brickyard, slaughterhouse, vegetable canning plant and two cotton gins. Rather than being a drain on the system, Parchman supplied the state with net revenue of $825,000 as early as 1918. With 1200 prisoners supplying free labor for the farm, Parchman became a role model for the concept of "Punishment for Profit." But the path to its success was paved with a dark history.

After slavery was abolished in the South, crime was redefined as an entire society adjusted to the abrupt disruption of plantation farming. A practice known as "convict leasing" was started in 1868 by a clever businessman named Edmund Richardson. Under this legal approach, men and women convicted of crimes were "leased" to local farmers, and ordered to serve their sentence by performing free labor.

Condemned by Northerners as merely an extension of slavery, this practice in fact did return many former slaves to bondage on the very plantations from which they were freed. The passage of the Mississippi Black Codes guaranteed a steady supply of "criminals," as they imposed fines for new "crimes" focusing on the newly freed black man. The Vagrancy Act declared that every negro over age 18 must show proof of a job at the beginning of every year. With thousands of former slaves now seeking employment, the chances of breaking this new law were extremely high. Having no job resulted in a $50.00 fine, which was virtually impossible to pay. They were then arrested and auctioned off to any white man who could pay their fine, with the amount being deducted from the negroes' "wages." Preference was often given to the former owner of the slave (see *"Worse Than Slavery"* by Rutgers history professor David M. Oshinsky).

Convict leasing ended in 1894, with the state's intent to

establish a prison farm. Parchman was born, and forced labor was now "in house." The controversy over convict leasing died, but in its death throes, new evils sprang forth. Described as "an isolated plantation with shotguns, whips and bloodhounds," Parchman Prison, over the next 60 years, earned the title bestowed on it by William Faulkner: DESTINATION DOOM. "Black Annie," the famous leather strip used to brutally whip prisoners, performed its power publicly, at the slightest provocation, on victims who were stripped and spread-eagle.

Prisoners armed with shotguns, known as "Trustee Shooters," had authority to shoot escaping convicts, a practice which was still in effect when I began working at the prison. Many claim that Parchman was also used as a threat, and sometimes a reality, to silence the civil rights workers of the 1960's who came to Mississippi for the marches and Freedom Rides. At one time, over 300 Freedom Riders were imprisoned at Parchman Prison Farm, and were often forced to work on the chain gang in the searing heat. Ross Barnett, the Governor of Mississippi, reportedly visited the farm several times to check on the activists, telling the guards to *"break their spirit, not their bones."*

With the majority of prisoners being black males, and the trials of infamous KKK terrorists glaring at the world, the longstanding brutalities of Parchman were increasingly revealed in headlines across the country.

Though I was oblivious to this "underworld" of my seemingly polite Southern society, this was indeed the Parchman whose gates I entered with my church group that day in 1965, filled with only a slight apprehension and a vague notion of "making a difference."

NOTE: Significant changes to Mississippi's entire penal system came in 1972, by order of William C. Keady, a federal judge from Mississippi. Today, minimum and medium-custody inmates still work in the fields as part of the "Agricultural Enterprises" program at Parchman farm, as well as at the South Mississippi prison, helping with the planting, harvesting and processing of okra, corn, cabbages, squash, peppers, pecans, rice and more. The prison agricultural program (commonly referred to as MPAE) also still runs a livestock swine operation, a feed mill and a poultry facility. In the fiscal year 2012, there were an average of 300 inmates working per month in the MPAE program, which equaled 75,000 man days. Based on 8 hours per day for 250 work days, this equates to 600,000 hours that the inmates were engaged in productive labor, resulting in a profit for the state and a self-supporting supply of food for inmates.

Chapter Two

Entry Granted

The sign read, "For the Next Two Miles Stop Only for Emergencies." We were within moments of entering the Parchman compound, and a shiver went all the way through me. "I am really going into the unknown," I realized, feeling like a missionary entering a foreign country. Prisons are indeed functioning societies of their own, and my instincts immediately told me to view Parchman as a separate cultural entity.

Insects from the surrounding farmlands splattered on our windshield as we covered the remaining miles of scorched grass and dust in the searing heat of the Mississippi Delta summer day. Arriving at the fairly innocuous prison entrance, the sign at the gate announced simply, "Mississippi State Penitentiary." The leader of our group showed the required letter of clearance, and the barricade was lifted. I remember feeling surprised that we were not frisked or searched in any way.

Our destination was Camp Seven, one of the many dingy old buildings approximately seven miles into the heart of the prison farm. Inside the gates, the acres and acres of farmland resembled the usual Delta terrain. With housing "camps" dotted throughout, it was not at all how I had pictured a state penitentiary. The prison officials had their personal residences on the farm, and their homes lined the road we traveled on the way to Camp Seven. We could see prisoners mowing yards or walking from place to place, seemingly with no supervision. In my naiveté, I thought it would be easy for them to escape. I was yet to learn of the K-Nine Unit of bloodhounds or the Trustee Shooters, and hadn't thought about the remote and isolated location of Parchman.

Continuing further, we passed a camp that was identified to me as the hospital. Several elderly men in wheelchairs, and various others on benches under sparse trees, played cards and dominoes. They stared blankly as I waved to them. Their less-than-enthusiastic response was attributed to a rule forbidding them to interact with a "free world" lady. I was suddenly glad that I had been admonished not to wear my usual short skirts, then in fashion. Clad in a frumpy looking ankle-length skirt borrowed from an older lady, I hoped that none of my country-club friends had seen me before we left the city limits. But I was now aware that a mere glimpse of someone from the outside must be refreshing, whatever they were wearing.

Several towers dotted the landscape, silhouetting the heads of security guards swinging rhythmically back and forth, scanning the countryside. Looming in the horizon, back from the main road, tall steel fences were topped with a tangle of razor wire, encircling a dreary looking red brick building. The sign announced "Maximum Security."

The afternoon sun lit the razor wire with a brilliant silver gleam. Though ominous, it also appeared beautiful to me that day, not unlike a bright halo. My companions explained to me that Maximum Security housed the gruesome gas chamber, as well as Death Row convicts and Escape Risk convicts. In addition, the most difficult and provocative inmates were housed there in Solitary Confinement. I would one day become very familiar with the sight of lone individuals in single cells with iron bars, an image that I, as an average non-offender, had previously seen only through the eyes of Hollywood movie producers.

We finally arrived at Camp Seven, parked the car, and gave our keys to a guard. We entered what I still recall today as a miserable roach-infested building. We were then ushered into a dining room that reeked of unidentifiable odors, and someone unceremoniously yelled, *"CHURCH!"*

A large group of "colored" men, many with scowling faces, straggled in – and my first of future thousands of prison church services came to life. The camps were still segregated in 1965, and the assembling black convicts were sullenly, but quietly, hostile to the group of white church folks who dragged them from their few hours of rest to attend the mandatory services. I sat beside one young man who dared to whisper, *"I hate you people."* I was a bit uneasy, thinking that my preacher had not quite prepared me for this. But I also understood; would I myself want to be forced to attend church against my will?

Several years later, when Christ became real in my own life, I learned from the Apostle Paul to *"become all things to all men so that by all possible means I might save some"* (I Corinthians 9:22b).

In the 30 years I spent as a volunteer and a chaplain in two Mississippi prisons, my practice became one of "winning" people. To both staff and convicts alike who experienced relationship problems in the prison, my advice became *"don't fight them – win them."* On this initial visit, however, my only concern was to be kind and friendly, and to get through it in the best way I could.

After the service ended, we were allowed to mingle with the prisoners, until the guard yelled, *"COUNT!"* This indicated that it was time for us to leave and the men to be accounted for. The convicts I interacted with were well-mannered, calling me "Ma'am" and expressing curiosity over my reason for coming. They were unaccustomed to having anyone genuinely care for their well being, particularly "white folks" in a segregated Southern state.

All I had to give them that day was my own kind nature, along with some Christian lingo I had adopted as part of my "churchianity." The knowledge I had in my head appeared useful to them in some way, even though the reality of Christ was not yet in my own heart.

I left the prison that day glowing with the satisfaction of having done my good works. I couldn't wait to report my experience to my family and to the church. Upon arriving home, my husband muttered, *"Don't tell them you're married to a lawyer,"* and my four children begged for full descriptions of real live convicts. The church applauded my bravery, and I became hooked. I was now a regular member of "the Parchman Team." Saturday nights were still reserved for the country club, but on Sunday afternoons, I now went to prison.

II Corinthians 13:5 :
"Examine yourself to see if you are in the faith…"

How could I have been fooled for so long
into thinking that I was a Christian?
Thank God that He began to draw me unto Himself.

Chapter Three

Humble Beginnings

Country clubs and prisons – black and white – war and peace – sinner and saint – balancing precariously between the extremes has been such a part of my life that it is no longer intimidating. The first experience of a rapid transition in my life's direction came very early, at the age of five.

I was born Wendy Dorothy Burrage, in Leigh-On-Sea, a small fishing village near London in the county of Essex, England. The year was 1934, the same one in which Adolph Hitler became Fuhrer of Germany. Europe had recuperated from WWI, and ordinary families such as my own had little reason to recognize the ominous signs that the world was on its next collision course towards the chaos of WWII.

I was the first child of Bill and Queenie Burrage, as adorable in my father's eyes as I was precocious in my mother's. I commanded their full affection, until forced to share center stage three years later with the birth of my brother, Ted. Having contracted the dreaded polio at birth, he spent much of his first years in the hospital. Our sibling ties, however, were fully strengthened in later years as he gallantly defeated my "enemies" by kicking them with his iron leg braces.

By today's standards, we would be considered a poor family, with ordinary ancestors, all of whom were working class citizens. On my mother's side, she and her six siblings survived on my grandfather's wages as a tram driver, until his early death in a work-related accident. Their mother, my "Nanny Nell", took in ironing as the sole means of supporting the family until the children reached working age.

My father's childhood was equally as subsistent, but decidedly more adventurous. He and his eight siblings spent their formative years in London, moving from place to place, two steps ahead of collection agents. Their dad (my grandfather "Gandy") was famous for his get-rich-quick schemes, and the children never knew when they would be required to hastily throw their belongings into a suitcase and dash off to a new identity. It's a miracle that my father grew up to be the responsible, caring and secure parent he consistently was throughout my childhood.

Though I was too young to know the full implications it brought, war and it's monstrous allies of pain, poverty and separation soon invaded my young world. Before the war started, we moved temporarily to Coventry for Dad to find work. It happened that, second only to London, Coventry was one of the most bombed cities in England, due to its airplane factories. German bombs whistling and bursting were a common occurrence, with delayed-action torpedoes and unexploded incendiary devices able to demolish an entire street in an instant. These vehicles of airborne arson claimed St. Michaels, the cherished Coventry Cathedral, as well as King Henry VIII Grammar School. The city center practically disappeared amidst the vast destruction of ancient Medieval architecture, leaving concrete skeletons in place of the department stores and small shops along Butcher Row and Pepper Lane. All gone forever. There was eventually little gas, water or electricity, and food was in short supply.

Daddy was sent overseas to fight with the British Army, my Mummy joined thousands of other women in factories to contribute to the war effort, and little brother Ted was still in the hospital being treated for polio. I was soon to learn my own fate.

I was five years old when I became an "evacuee," herded onto a bus with a nametag and a Mickey Mouse gas mask, headed to the countryside of Staffordshire. Thousands of young children like me were wrenched from the arms of their parents and families and transferred out of the cities, away from the danger of German bombs (similar to the children in "The Chronicles of Narnia" by C.S. Lewis). Only when I became a mother did I understand what a difficult decision that must have been for my own mother.

Upon arrival in the village of Two Gates in Staffordshire, our weary group of little evacuees, on our own without mums and dads for the first time ever, stumbled off the bus into the chaos of being assigned to new families. Refusing to let fate make the decision for me, I pointed to the family I wanted and stubbornly insisted, *"I want THAT family."* And I got them!

For over four years, I lived away with the Wain family, far from my own loved ones. "Auntie" and "Uncle" Wain, a coal miner, along with their son Keith, took me in and nurtured me as their own, making a lasting impression on my life. There are many stories of abuse, neglect and lifelong scars associated with the displacement of British children during those wartime years. I was fortunate, however, to be sheltered by a loving family.

Our food supply was limited and ration books mandatory, but with the potato fields nearby, and the pigs in the back yard, we weren't as deprived as city dwellers. We children "scrumped" (English slang for mischievous stealing) apples and gooseberries, and scoured the countryside for blackberries and chestnuts in season. Once a week we had an egg, and what a treat that was! Occasionally, American servicemen appeared and we followed them like the Pied Piper, chanting, *"Got any gum, chum?"* These "Yanks" were our only source of coveted chocolate and gum.

The occasional visits home to Mummy in Coventry were thrilling to me, and the highlights were the nights spent sleeping in the air raid shelter. The government provided a metal shed to every household, positioned at the end of the garden, to which we would run at the sound of the sirens. These igloo-shaped metal sheds were placed above holes dug four feet into the ground and usually covered with earth that was often used for a small vegetable patch. Cautiously peeping out, with the whistling of bombs in the quiet darkness, we would catch glimpses of German planes caught in the searchlights, or descending parachutes and the "barrage balloons" by the hundreds to keep enemy airplanes from flying low. Mummy was fearless, dashing back and forth between the house and the shelter to make tea, protected from falling shrapnel by a lone cake tin on her head.

Toward the end of the war, Mummy and brother Ted moved back to our beloved hometown of Leigh-On-Sea, a fishing village on the Thames Estuary about 30 miles from London. At the age of 10, after nearly five years at Two Gates, I was reunited with my family and moved into my grandmother's tiny cottage on the seafront, with no running water and no inside toilet. Narrow cobblestone streets wound their way through our now-historic neighborhood, with ramshackle wooden sheds hawking cockles, mussels, whelks, winkles, shrimp and jellied eels from the waters just feet away.

I thrived in the salty sea air and in the company of the fishermen, many of whom were my relatives. They became my constant companions as I helped them mend their nets, sharing their big hunks of bread and cheese. I sat contentedly for hours, talking to the "old salts" or joining them before sunrise in their days' work of shrimping or cockling onboard the traditional bawley boats.

These small fishing-smacks were unique to the coasts of Kent and Essex, many being built right there in Leigh by locals, including my neighbor, Barry. Constructed with a boomless cutter-rig, they were easily brailed up when working the trawl nets. They stretched a mere 40 feet long and had half a deck, with a wet well to keep the fish alive. Before returning to shore, the shrimp were cooked onboard in a boiler, ready to be sold at the stalls along the front. A tiny staircase led to the bowels of the boat, where I sneaked down for a spoonful of condensed milk or a biscuit (cookie) before rejoining the crew to help haul in the day's catch before the tide went out and stranded us in the mud.

Many of these fishermen had volunteered their small boats to aid in the Evacuation of Dunkirk, a rescue operation which lifted about 340,000 Allied troops from the coast of France in 1940. The larger Naval ships, destroyers and barges were finding it difficult to maneuver into the coves and harbors of Dunkirk, where thousands upon thousands of soldiers – British, French and Belgian – were stranded and being attacked by the Germans. The privately-owned pleasure and fishing boats, often with their owners aboard, were the only hope for getting in close enough.

J.B. Priestly, a wartime public broadcaster, praised these humble heroes who *"...sailed into the inferno, to defy bombs, shells, magnetic mines, torpedoes, machine gun fire – to rescue our soldiers"* (Postscript broadcast, June 5th, 1940). One tale, still retold in historical accounts, relates the courage and determination of a 17-year-old boy from Leigh-On-Sea who was denied the chance to join the fishing boats headed to France because he was too young. He dashed home for written permission from his parents and then ran for miles along the English coastline to catch up with his "fleet" of fishing boats as they prepared to cross the channel for France. One local fishing boat, the *Renown*, sank after hitting a German mine, and two of the Osborne boys, Lukie and Frankie, never made it back home to Leigh-on-Sea.

To the world at large, the significance of evacuating 340,000 soldiers from the French seaport of Dunkirk was enormous. To me, as a relatively insignificant young child, the evacuation meant life itself, for one reason: my dear Daddy, Bill Burrage, was on those shores of Dunkirk, valiantly fighting for his life and the lives of those around him, against the evils of Hitler and Nazi Germany. Though his rescue boat was torpedoed, he was eventually evacuated, along with thousands of others, in that fateful week of May 28th through June 4th, 1940.

The rescue was brilliantly successful, but the war raged on. The Allied forces had suffered a debilitating defeat at Dunkirk and were forced to abandon the vast majority of its tanks, artilleries, equipment and transportation vehicles in retreat. Just across the English Channel, families like mine all across Britain were in grave danger. My dad stayed on to continue fighting Hitler and the German aggression. He did not return home to us in Leigh-On-Sea until the war ended in 1945, though he faithfully wrote and mailed fairy tales, stories and letters to my brother Ted and me, to that I, equally faithfully, replied. After Daddy's death in the 1980's I found letters from "little" Wendy in his desk.

In the last months of the war, living so close to London, we occasionally went into the city to check on my aunt, and had to dash into the underground (subway) when the sirens started screaming that an attack was imminent. That too, for a child, was an adventure to be remembered in my old age. Back in Leigh-on-Sea, there were some alarming times as well, ducking under boats or the nearest shelters when German V-2 rockets exploded nearby. Developed by the German scientist Wernher von Braun, the V-2 was the world's first ballistic missile, which traveled faster than the speed of sound, at 3,600 mph, and could deliver a warhead from more that 200 miles away.

The ones being fired at us were likely launched from Holland (which had surrendered to the Nazis) and took only five minutes to reach us. They could not be intercepted, and more than 1000 V-2s were fired against Britain. We called them "buzz bombs" or "doodlebugs," and even the tiniest children understood that when their buzzing noise stopped, that meant they were coming down. Once, as we played on the beach, a V-2 rocket stopped overhead, then exploded on a small island nearby.

Little did I know that, many years after the war, the spare parts from these same V-2 rockets manufactured by the Nazis would be used by America to develop the space programs that took the first Americans into orbit – or that I would be in ministry at Parchman Penitentiary in the Mississippi Delta, as an American citizen, on the day in 1969 when the first man landed on the moon.

The war finally ended, and we celebrated V-E (Victory in Europe) Day on May 8th, 1945. The black-out blankets were removed from windows, the streetlights came on for the first time in years, and neighborhoods all over England blocked off traffic to celebrate with street parties, food, and speeches. Since I had little recollection of life before the war, everything was wonderland, bright and beautiful, especially when my dear Daddy Bill came home!

After years apart, we were practically strangers, but we spent many hours becoming reacquainted. He told me stories about his campaigns in Italy, France and Africa. I am sure there were intense and terrifying experiences that I will never know about, for the tales he chose for us children were entertaining and light and humorous. My favorite was the story of when he dropped General Montgomery's meal of Spam in the mud and hurriedly washed it off before serving it to the famous army leader. The funniest tale that my gifted storytelling Daddy told us was when his convoy stopped at a French farm outhouse only to find that it had no roof, and the farm occupants were watching from an upstairs window.

The remainder of my childhood went by pleasantly enough. My parents scraped up enough money to open an ice cream parlor, which was very popular in a community of people who appreciated the simplest of pleasures. After years of wartime poverty and deprivation, towns all over England adjusted to peace and everyday life.

Being a very class-oriented society, the working class families like my own were very conscious of their lower status in society. For its duration, WWII proved to be an equalizer in Britain; all were welcomed in the fight against Hitler. Huddled together in air raid shelters as the German Luftwaffe dropped bombs nightly, it made little difference whether we were wealthy or noble, or one of the masses. In the light of survival, every person was equal in their ability to contribute, as well as in their fight for life and liberty.

Our society would never be quite the same again after the war, but lasting change does come slowly, and I distinctly remember feeling inferior or unimportant in the world. Our family lived as millions of others, in obscurity, looked upon by the upper classes as insignificant – and often treated that way. I see these humble beginnings of mine now as a foundational part of God's plan for my future. No parts of our lives are wasted or unrelated or without value to a God who puts it all together.

This early exposure to issues of equality and class systems prepared me, though unconsciously, for the socially volatile times in which I would live my early adulthood in America. Civil rights issues were raging in the South by the time I arrived there as the young bride of a Navy Lieutenant.

I met my future husband in Spain, where I had gone on my first unchaperoned trip abroad, at the age of 18. For months, I saved portions from my salary working at a newspaper in London, then booked a trip to the sleepy little town of Tarragona, near the larger city of Barcelona. My friend, Eve, and I arrived there one day before the American Sixth Fleet docked in the harbor.

As the sailors and marines filled the town with their enthusiastic energy after six weeks at sea, it became apparent that this would be a vacation to remember. One young man, an officer wearing his dress whites, captivated me with his soft Southern drawl as he asked, *"Do you speak English?"* My reply was a haughty, *"I AM English!"* He laughed, I smiled, and we were inseparable for the next week. I dined aboard his ship, surrounded by the first Americans I had met since I was a young child in the WWII years. A week later, his ship departed for the USA and I returned to my life in England – but my life would change drastically. We wrote for two years and spent one Christmas together in Leigh-On-Sea, before being married in the beautiful 13th century church of St. Clements at the top of Leigh Hill.

Only days after our wedding, we embarked for America on a military plane, landing in Maryland. Before reporting for duty in Boston, we set off for Mississippi in what I considered to be the biggest car ever made, a 1954 Dodge sedan. I was going to "meet the family," totally oblivious to the world that awaited me.

Chapter Four

The Clash

"Confusion Culture Conversation"

To say that I experienced culture shock in Mississippi would be an understatement. The historian James Cobb has dubbed the Mississippi Delta *"the most Southern place on earth,"* and I was soon to find out what that meant.

I arrived in a wool suit over a woolen sweater to what was surely the hottest, stickiest and most humid weather anywhere on the planet. I eventually discovered this was not even summer; there was worse to come! Air conditioners were so new that few homes were as yet equipped with them. Instead, fans merely stirred together the hot air and the swarms of insects, creating a suffocating wet blanket that hung over me constantly.

For the reception planned by my new in-laws, I could not wear my wedding dress due to the heat, and I had no clothing that would otherwise fit with the climate or culture of my new surroundings. In the receiving line, I understood very few of the words spoken to me in the strange drawl that is still uniquely "Southern," and I was overwhelmed by the multitude of invitations to *"come see us."* It wasn't until after I had run myself ragged trying to visit all these people that I realized it was more a polite thing to say than it was a specific invitation. I held my fork wrong, didn't know I was supposed to call my elders "ma'am" and "sir," and had no idea that the black faces in the kitchen were servants and not allowed to speak unless spoken to.

My in-laws lived on the Delta Pine and Land Company in Scott, Mississippi, the largest plantation in the state. It basically was run under a sharecropping system for many years, as were most of the former slave plantations in the Delta. The entire town was owned by the plantation, and my husband's father ran the company store.

It was the levee near Scott that broke in 1927, causing the infamous Mississippi River flood that swamped the Delta in up to 15 feet of water covering about 30 miles wide and 100 miles long. Identified afterward as the Mound Landing Crevasse, this crack in the levee grew to 3,000 feet wide and dumped about 470,000 cubic feet of muddy Mississippi

River water into the Delta, turning plantations into watery graves and lakes. The Delta Pine and Land Company lost 600 acres to the flood, with the land now covered in gritty sand and mud.

By the 1940s, the decade before I arrived there, the plantation had recovered and benefited from labor by German prisoners during WWII, who were shipped to America after their capture in North Africa by American and British forces. These members of Hitler's once-famous Afrika Corps now labored in the hot Delta sun, picking cotton and planting trees. Mechanical pickers were not yet invented, so the cotton was picked by hand. In the spring, they chopped away the weeds from tender young plants, then in the autumn methodically pulled the cotton from the bolls, one by one, filling canvas bags and dragging them through the dirt fields as they grew heavier and heavier. By the time I arrived in 1954, the German labor had been replaced with "colored" field hands.

Officials from the plantation, which was partially owned by British investors, had been guests at my wedding in England, arriving in fancy top hats and expensive suits to sit amongst the fishermen and working class shop owners who were my friends and family.

Though none of us would ever have imagined it at the time, the Delta Pine and Land Company eventually become one of the largest cotton seed breeders in the entire world, and united with the Monsanto corporation in a $1.5 billion merger. Along with the United States Department of Agriculture, Delta Pine and Land developed the controversial genetic engineering technology that makes sterile seeds, condemned today by some as a way of forcing farmers to buy new biotech seeds each year rather than saving the seed from one year's crop to plant the next.

When I arrived there, Scott seemed like just a small, dusty company-owned town with a lazy strip of four or five stores spanning about 100 feet, surrounded by miles and miles of endless cotton fields. It felt to me like the end of civilization.

Though it was the year 1954, and equality among the races was a constitutional ideal, the reality was far from it. The famous Supreme Court ruling of *Brown vs Board of Education*, which made segregation illegal, was handed down only a couple of weeks before I arrived there. Everything was still segregated...drinking fountains, doctor's offices, movie theaters, restaurants, swimming pools, churches, and schools. And they would remain that way for many years, as new state laws were constantly created to counteract the Federal ruling. The Ku Klux Klan was prominent at the time, and my new family wisely withheld from me the fact that one of the family was once an active member of the clan.

My husband failed to see the impact of this start to my new life, so far away from the fresh sea air of Leigh-On-Sea and the people who loved and understood me. After two years as a Navy wife, and when he finished his law degree at the University of Mississippi, I nonetheless began to feel more comfortable.

My first journey home to see my family in 1956 was with my first newborn son, John, then only four months old, onboard the Queen Elizabeth steamship, and returning on its sister-ship the Queen Mary. The journey took six days of pitching and churning over icy February ocean waves, with me violently ill the entire time. I remember the voyage vividly, but was unable to benefit from the luxury of these famous ships.

Once air travel became more common, I would gather up what was by that time my four young children, each one less than two years apart in age, and make the arduous journey to New York and then 13 hours over the Atlantic Ocean on a relatively small plane by today's standards. Though the first prop-jets began crossing the North Atlantic in 1958, it was much longer before jets were transformed into the sleek, efficient modes of transportation that we know today. At least three of my four children were throwing up every hour or so along the journey. In the days of formal dress for traveling, this was a challenge! What would I have done if my 6-year-old firstborn child had not been the kind, capable and helpful child who has now become an adult with the same traits?

In my new home in the Mississippi Delta, I found myself identifying much more easily with the "inferiors" in the kitchen or the fields. As my husband progressed in his chosen field of law over the next few years, I would constantly be required to exhibit social graces and skills that did not come naturally to me. I was determined, however, to "fit in" and to make my new husband proud of me, so I began to listen and to watch this society of people very carefully.

One of the first things I noticed about Southern people is that they all attended church – a lot. Everyone identified themselves as Christian, and church participation was expected as a part of the culture. To be successful and influential, it was an unwritten requirement. I was frequently asked, *"What church do you belong to?"* I had no idea what that meant. I would honestly reply, *"the Church of England,"* since the United Kingdom is a church state, and citizens are naturally born into that church. I had never been to church, except to weddings, funerals or christenings, and don't recall knowing anyone else who ever did. I had never heard the gospel and never known a Christian.

The fact that there was no religious training whatsoever in my background would have been unimaginable to the typical Southerner of that generation. Eudora Welty, the Pulitzer Prize winning author from Mississippi, once wrote about the power of place in forming our perceptions: *"Place absorbs our earliest notice...It bestows on us our original awareness."* Certainly a more striking example of this would be hard to find, as I lived in the midst of these people, as much a product of my own past environment as they were of theirs.

As I now watched these Christians to see how I was supposed to behave, I discovered them to be no different than any of the people with whom I grew up. The one exception was that they all attended church services. So I joined a church with my husband and determined that if I was going to be a "Christian," then I would be a really good one – and an active one. After a while, I taught Sunday School classes, held many offices in women's organizations, directed

Summer Bible School, worked with the youth, and attended all church functions.

As our four children arrived, they were immediately taken to church, and I faithfully involved them in the multitude of activities. By then, I had learned all the Christian words and convinced myself that I was a Christian. It never occurred to me that there was anything missing. I was performing what I knew to be the correct religious duties and thought that all was well with my soul.

The winds of change do not always start as cool, cleansing breezes. More commonly, they begin with either restless stirrings that build in time – or they rush in with the force of devastating tornadoes. I have experienced both in my lifetime, in equal portions. My husband's legal career flourished and we rose to social heights – but our marriage deteriorated rapidly. We both poured our energies into committees, country clubs and social events, none of which filled the void in my life that I called a "bad marriage." I tried to find comfort in buying "stuff," attending numerous parties and traveling, none of which provided any lasting satisfaction.

The void in my life, and the constant striving to fill it, seemed to parallel the civil and racial disturbances that were erupting around me. The unrest of an entire generation gathered momentum and threatened to rip the foundation of our cultivated society. The black faces in the kitchens and cotton fields of the Delta were no longer subservient and passive, as the Civil Rights revolution demanded that souls be purged and truth be revealed. Hypocrisy, inequality, and injustice in the American South were spread out for the world to see.

After two years in the Navy, we had settled in at Oxford, Mississippi, for my husband to finish his law degree at "Ole Miss" University. Less than five years later, Ole Miss drew the attention of the world for its refusal to allow black students to register for classes. U.S. Marshalls and Federal troops were summoned to escort James Meredith onto the campus, while State troopers blocked their progress. The campus exploded that autumn when thousands of U.S. soldiers clashed with students and townspeople in the infamous campus riot that brought gunfire, tear gas and bloodshed to our institution of Higher Learning.

By the time the Civil Rights Act was signed into law by President Johnson in 1964, my husband was an established member of the legal community in the Delta, and was often consulted in the conflicts resulting from the Mississippi Freedom Summer marches and confrontations. Fannie Lou Hamer was beaten nearly to death as she tried to register to vote in 1963, only a few miles from where we lived. That same year, I paid the mandated $3 voting poll tax that was created in Mississippi to keep black people from registering to vote and having their voices heard. Three civil rights activists were murdered in our part of the state, while Medgar Evers was gunned down about three hours away in the state capital of Jackson. As President of the local school board, my husband fought to come up with peaceful solutions to curb the violence and rioting common all over the state during the eventual integration of the public schools. Curfews were common, tensions were high, and revolt roared on both sides of the color line.

Though history in its larger context was being written in every corner of the Delta, my own transformation was larger, and immensely more significant to me, on a personal level. As the discontent in my life deepened, my friends, all of whom were church people, tried to comfort me. However, nobody prayed with me or suggested there might be a spiritual solution. Day after miserable day, year after miserable year, my unhappiness continued and despair deepened.

Finally one day, in my agony I sat down alone at home and said, *"I give up."* It was more than just words; it was a cry of desperation and an acknowledgement that I could not remove the hurt I was feeling. I did not consciously call out to God, but He knew my need and responded in what I now see as a dramatic and miraculous way, much like the experience of the apostle Paul, designed to make this unaware woman understand that there was more to Christianity than I had experienced.

As I sat alone in the family room, the Lord Jesus Christ came to me and touched me, filling me with light and waves of joy. The misery that had filled my life for so many years was lifted, and I felt breathless with wonder and excitement. The Good News came to me, one spiritually poor and desperately needy. I saw with a new spiritual dimension to life, and the relief I felt as He took my burdens was immense. The Savior who I had known only intellectually entered into my heart to give me a totally new life.

I could not have explained, as I now understand from years of studying the Scripture, that God's Spirit had given me a new birth. However, in my stunned realization that He was in the room, I managed to say, *"Lord, I give you my life. I want to go where you send me, be what you want me to be, and do what you want me to do."*

I had no idea then that His desire was to send me to prison.

Chapter Five

Parchman

"Ain't but the one thing that I done wrong,
Stayed in Mississippi just a day too long."

"Negro Prison Songs" Rounder Records, 1974
Bob Dylan 1998, Recorded by Sheryl Crow

I quickly realized that my visits to Parchman had taken on new meaning. What had once been just a church activity now became a calling on my heart. Things changed drastically after my conversion experience, and nearly everyone in my social circles, including the church, labeled me a religious fanatic. One rumor even claimed that I had a nervous breakdown. To the individual who reported that to me I said, *"If that's what this is, everyone should have one."* My desire to "shout it from the rooftops" was less than well received! Fortunately, God did not leave me to stand alone with my new convictions and fervor for Him; other born-again believers began to emerge and pull me into their circles, nurturing and teaching me from His word.

In spite of what was perceived as my previous lack of interest in spiritual matters, I was invited to attend a neighborhood prayer group, led by my now long-time friend Ann Woods. Ann agrees that it had to be God, because they were most hesitant to include me. I was so excited to find other women who understood what had happened to me.

I applied, and was given permission, to visit Parchman more frequently. I discovered that I now had more than my own goodness to offer these captives, outcast from society and imprisoned by their own sin and its consequences. I now knew that freedom comes from a place inside, and the key that opens the gates to a new life is Jesus Christ himself. Whether the bars that hold us are physical, mental or spiritual, we are all equal in God's eyes – and all stand in need of redemption.

God gives us personalities that equip us for our place in the world. My very overt style of communicating the gospel was undoubtedly fashioned more for hardened criminals than for genteel and polite society. My pastor at the time, Dr. Wilson Benton, was besieged by complaining church members who tired of what they perceived as my critical spirit. He cautioned me from the Scriptures to be *"wise as a serpent and gentle as a dove."* Wisdom comes with patience, and from patience, understanding. I was to learn both – but not from the church. Very soon I was to be working full time, day after day, and eventually from night into darkness, at the prison.

Though I fought earnestly to save my troubled marriage, my husband filed for divorce, leaving me as a single mother of four children and a volunteer job that provided no income, as I was at the time still a volunteer at Parchman. The answer to my prayers came in the form of a paycheck for secretarial skills that were dubious, at best! There was no official position at Parchman for an Assistant Chaplain, but an overwhelming need for one. Chaplain Glenn Howell creatively found the solution by hiring me as a secretary and giving me training, and then gradually increasing my responsibilities to include ministering to the female prisoners.

The chaplain's office was located in Camp Three, which was also the male pre-release center. We had the opportunity to spend time with the prisoners who were soon to be reunited with the world-at-large. There were also convicts who were housed there on a permanent basis, working in the kitchen, janitorial offices, and other assignments.

As a working prison farm in the 1960s and 70s, Parchman provided its own food, and jobs were plentiful. Many prisoners worked in the fields or on maintenance crews, and the more privileged ones were assigned as servants to the personnel living on the grounds of the prison. Some of the female convicts worked as cooks or babysitters, and the Warden himself had both house and yard convicts. The men in the K-Nine units lived in their own camp, disliked and mistrusted by their fellow convicts. They had more freedom of movement and extra privileges, typically for training and managing the dogs used to chase escapees. The infamous convict "trustee shooters" were always ready (and some more than willing) to exercise their right to shoot anyone trying to gain their freedom illegally. To walk past the painted gun-line of wide, white stripes surrounding each camp was equal to declaring, "*I want to be shot.*" There was much abuse in this method of controlling the inmates, and it was not unusual to hear of provocation to cross the line.

Though I never personally witnessed it, I was often told of the beatings and cruel treatment that the prisoners received at the hands of the guards. I did on occasion see convicts chained to fences and as I became acquainted with the personalities of some of these guards, I did believe them capable of evil. Even after the Federal Court got involved and instituted great changes, it was not unusual to hear of convicts being beaten in soundproof rooms. Though it was normally done in a manner that hid the scars, one of the girls once showed me her bruises. I reported the incident, but a convict's word is seldom sufficient, and I had no irrefutable proof to substantiate her claims.

The housing camps, for the most part, were bug and rat infested old buildings. Elaborate homemade "traps" were concocted by the inmates to triumph over the rodents. Having grown up in the much colder climate of the United Kingdom, I had not yet overcome my horror of what I still call "Mississippi Critters." My good intentions of sitting at the bedsides of the female convicts during counseling were forever waylaid by the scampering of roaches across the bedsheets.

Dingy and ugly are the best words to describe these housing camps. The women made pathetic attempts to bring a touch of beauty into their "home" with artificial flowers and hand-drawn pictures. The ugliness loomed even larger in contrast, and their efforts merely added to the overall sadness of the building.

My bedside conversations with the women, in the only semblance of personal space left to them, most often revealed stories of children, home, favorite recipes, universal bonds between females of every age, race, and creed. With these particular women, however, the consequences of their crimes were a total loss of all they held dear in life. Ranging from embezzlement to homicide, I understood that with their crimes came a need for punishment. However, I also understood the ache of guilt and loneliness. By God's grace, I did have the answer for them, which was forgiveness through Christ. Many found great joy and purpose in life, even as they remained in physical bondage to the State for their sin and crime.

Though we did not realize it at the time, Chaplain Howell, in sending me to these women in their camps, was training me to be a chaplain. He was also teaching me, by word and example, how to successfully merge compassion and love with an intolerance for transgression. Forgiveness does not mean an exemption from the consequences of sin. In my desire to help convicts, I resolved to never lose sight of the victims involved in their crimes. It is a common misconception that all Christians are soft on crime. I recall being excused from jury duty because the prosecution assumed that my faith would not allow for justice. He failed to understand that God's love is frequently tough because He wants the best for us. However, the same God who said that the wages of sin is death, also *"sent his only begotten Son into the world that whoever believes in Him shall have everlasting life."* (John 3:16 KJV).

Many of the females began to understand this, and to know Christ in a personal way. They were eager to know more about the One who had given them a new beginning and a hope for their future. Bible studies became a regular part of my day, though the spiritual changes in the prisoners were not always welcomed or understood by the guards and other employees. The female pre-release administrator, Bonnie Abels, defended me on several occasions, wisely acknowledging the transformation in "her girls." I thank her to this day for having the eyes to see God's hand at work.

Back in our office at Camp Three, Chaplain Howell kept things lively. Though a resolutely dedicated chaplain, he could easily have pursued a career in the theater. On many occasions, I would be in earnest conversation on the telephone with who I thought was an elderly woman, only to have "her" erupt in laughter, revealing the very male voice of my boss. He was a master impersonator, and used his humor to lighten what could easily have been a stressful and tragically sad daily job. He delighted in mimicking our Californian Warden, known to address female employees as "babe." Imagine my embarrassment the day I told the Warden, over the telephone, to "*shut up*" – only to discover that this time it really was the Warden, rather than the chaplain playing masquerade yet again.

In those first days and years at Parchman, as I stumbled my way through the ins-and-outs of prison life, God's "family" at Camp Three grew together. In later years, I would earn the nickname of "Ma" amongst the prisoners, and the seeds of this maternal role could be seen even from the beginning. One of my first experiences with the protective tendencies of the convicts on my behalf came from Israel Bradley at Camp Three.

Israel was serving two life sentences for murder. He worked in the kitchen at Camp Three, and we talked often. In the more than 25 years that I was to know Israel, he never tried to make excuses for his crime, nor did he complain about unjust treatment. One evening, as I prayed with a group of inmates after a Bible study, Israel observed a convict whispering something to me that was somewhat inappropriate. Israel later told me, "*Don't worry; it won't happen again.*" And it didn't. I never saw the offender again, and I never asked the guys how they handled it.

I judged Israel to be genuinely concerned about living his life to please God, quietly demonstrating his faith. After about 40 years serving time in a Mississippi prison, with little hope of ever regaining physical freedom, he was finally buried there.

Like Israel, there were many other young Christians being born into God's Kingdom at Parchman. If *"bloom where you are planted"* applies in these circumstances, then it is surely understandable that their growth would be tailored to their environment. How I rejoiced when a particularly tough man of the streets named Ray gave his life to Christ. Imagine my horror, however, when I discovered that Ray was using his physical strength to share the gospel. *"Ray, you cannot beat people into believing,"* I admonished.

*"They **will** listen to me,"* he replied.

It reminded me of the time when the disciples of Jesus wanted to "rain down thunder" on a Samaritan village because the people would not listen, but Jesus rebuked them (Luke 9:54).

Another new Christian, Barry, required medical treatment one day after refusing to defend himself against the physical attack of a fellow convict. Puzzled onlookers questioned, *"How come you're acting so weak?"* He replied simply that Jesus said to turn the other cheek.

I admired these baby Christians who suffered so much for their faith. One of the chaplain department's inmate helpers was abruptly sent to a notoriously tough camp for no apparent reason. Gifted with a gregarious personality, he brightened our lives and brought much joy before being taken away. As he steadfastly continued to live for his Savior in adverse conditions, his example influenced many and brought hope to the hopeless. Others began to change because of the influence of these convicts, and I think about their courage even now when I am required to make an unpopular stand.

People have asked me if there were any cases of the stereotypical "jailhouse religion" in Parchman. Sometimes, yes. One day I rushed into the office, excited to share my experience of praying with Marjorie, a large, rough, manipulative female serving a sentence for homicide. *"I sure wouldn't close my eyes around Marjorie,"* Chaplain Howell muttered. *"The last time someone did that, she stabbed him with a pair of scissors."*

Also among the females was a young teenager incarcerated with a death sentence for the brutal murder of a young man. She was an extremely gifted actress, who could cry piously one minute and curse like a sailor the next. Her acts were to elicit sympathy and help from gullible volunteers or anyone who could lessen the severity of her circumstances.

Over the years, I would come to know the hearts, minds, and spirits of many people convicted of crimes against society. Sincerity is not a given or even a norm. Discernment, however, was a gift that God gave to me over the years, and experience cultivated my judgement. In daily association with convicts, truth becomes more easily apparent.

There was no razor wire around Camp Three, where our Chaplain's office was located, and Trustee convicts had some freedom of movement outside the building during the daytime. After their working hours, they could be seen wistfully gazing at the sky or the distant peach orchard, or strolling around the nearby pond. Many miles from public roads, surrounded by cotton fields, the danger of escape at

Parchman was minimal. But it did happen on occasion. One such time involved a man considered to be Mississippi's number one criminal, a man who was later to become our Chaplain's helper and my lifelong friend.

My friends were appalled to learn that I was working with *the* Tommy Tarrants. His shootouts with state law enforcement agencies and the FBI were highly publicized in the late 1960s, as he and school teacher Kathy Ainsworth attempted to bomb the home of Meyer Davidson, a Jewish businessman in Meridian, Mississippi. His terrorist activities with the Ku Klux Klan sprang from a warped indoctrination by his elders, who considered Jews dangerous and blacks inferior.

As reporter Jack Nelson recounts in his book, *Terror in the Night*, Tommy became a hit man for the Klan, and bombed the Temple Beth Israel in Jackson, Mississippi on September 18, 1967. The target was chosen as retaliation against Rabbi Nussbaum, a prominent Civil Rights activist. Nine months later, on June 19th, 1968, he and Kathy were ambushed as they attempted to bomb Meyer Davidson's home, in what some claim was a deliberate setup by the FBI to assassinate Tommy. Kathy was killed in the shootout, a bullet shattering her spine and leaving a hole in her neck. Tommy was severely wounded, shot several times with shotgun fire as he lay semi-conscious on the ground. He was sentenced to 30 years in the Mississippi State Penitentiary.

As an escape risk, Tommy's first prison home was a Maximum Security cell, where he spent a relatively short time, before the Warden transferred him to the hospital camp.

Several months later, he escaped. Tommy, with his wry humor, explained the circumstances to me later: "*I looked around and I didn't like the accommodations – so I left.*" He, along with two others, planned and executed an escape.

They fled to another county, where they were hidden in an isolated, wooded area, and supplied with army-grade weapons. Because of an informant in their midst, however, they were recaptured in another shootout. One of the escapees was killed, and the other two were returned to Maximum Security.

Months in a 6 x 9 ft. cell gave Tommy plenty of time to read. He sought the truth for the first time with an open mind. Ravaging the works of great philosophers and sociologists, he finally poured his energies into reading the Bible, given to him by his grandmother. The Bible was not new to Tommy, having previously read parts of it out of context, merely to reinforce his prejudices. This time, however, it was different. He was genuinely convicted of the evil of his previous lifestyle and gave his life to Jesus. Kneeling on the concrete floor of his tiny cell, with tears of repentance, he determined to pursue *this* Jew for the rest of his life.

Tommy was eventually baptized by Chaplain Howell in the prison lake. Many who heard about his conversion experience believed it was a deliberate lie to gain release. However, his change was obvious, and two years later, he was given Trustee status and eventually transferred to the Trustee Camp Three. He became a Chaplain's Helper and instructor in the pre-release program, teaching courses in drivers education and positive thinking. This tall, lanky, intelligent man, formerly a notorious domestic terrorist, was transformed into a follower of Jesus, my friend and a brother in Christ. After more than 30 years of serving his Lord, most would now agree that his change is genuine. He was freed from prison in 1976. He earned his Masters of Divinity degree in 1986, then a Doctorate in Christian Spirituality. He has been a full-time pastor, and President of the C.S. Lewis Institute in Washington D.C., where he now serves as Vice President for Ministry and Director of the Washington Area Fellows Program. His autobiography, *Conversion of a Klansman*, was published by Doubleday in 1979, and is scheduled for re-release soon. He also co-authored a book with famous Civil Rights leader John Perkins, titled, *He's My Brother* (Chosen Books, 1994).

While many who have a conversion experience during incarceration do go on to live successfully in the world after their release, the "return rate" for prisoners in general is very high. Even those with sincere desires to change their circumstances face enormous obstacles as newly released ex-convicts. Many have no family, no money, no job, and no skills. They are given wings and told to fly with their new freedom – but many simply do not know how.

On occasion, I prevailed upon my friends or a church to "adopt" a newly released offender. But the social gaps are often prohibitive and intimidating. One young man, who I would describe as a "street person," was adopted by a church whose members are predominantly educated and prosperous. Though their intentions were good and they gave according to their ability to perceive the needs, the young man never did adjust, and eventually returned to his former lifestyle. After three ex-offenders reverted to their old habits, the sheriff advised one of my friends, Walter Herbison, to carry a gun because of his involvement with my "gangsters." People began to immediately say "*NO*" when they heard my voice. I understood!

I wish I could say that I never lost heart and that I always joyfully persevered. With failure often on an equal footing with success, I would sometimes mutter to myself, "*I'll just stay home and avoid these battles.*" With friends who misunderstood, fellow employees who blocked my efforts, and criticism from the very ones I strove to help, there were occasions when I would think, "*That's it, I've had enough. I don't have to do this.*" But that still, small voice inside of me would whisper, answering, "*Yes, you do.*"

When I was a young believer, I thought that the words from Psalm 37:4, "*Delight yourself in the Lord and He will give you the desires of your heart*" meant that I could ask for anything I wanted. I came to understand, however, that when I delighted in Christ, *His* desires for me actually became my own desires. As my comprehension of the prisoners' long-term needs grew, so did my desire to receive the official title and the ministry privileges of a full-time chaplain, instead of a secretary and chaplain-in-training.

With this in mind, I became a board member of Beginning Again In Christ (BAIC), an aftercare prison ministry dedicated to enabling men and women who desired to re-enter society successfully. They offered temporary housing, taught them social skills and provided job opportunities. Vic, our inmate chaplain's helper at Camp Three, accepted the position of Director for the ministry upon his release from Parchman. Prevailing over his previous drug habit, for which he had served two years at Parchman, he finished college and seminary training, and dedicated his time to helping other ex-offenders re-establish themselves.

BAIC desired to have a permanent presence at Parchman in order to, among other things, interview prospective residents for the ministry's Halfway House. They received permission from the state to place a full-time Chaplain at Parchman to represent them. The pay was minimum and the hours long – but I accepted the job. I had already committed my life completely to God's work within the prison, but I could now do so in the full capacity of a chaplain, knowing that His grace would be extended by my own humble human hands to these men and women as they progressed from captivity to freedom.

Chaplain Howell had moved on to a prison in another part of the state, and Parchman's new State Chaplain, Ron Padgett, was struggling to keep up with the constantly increasing prison population on the farm. Years later, when I too became a Head Chaplain employed by the state, I often agonized over my inability to effectively minister to the oppressing spiritual needs of so many people. So I know the relief Ron must have felt when BAIC paid my salary and sent me to aid him in his job. In my opinion, the Mississippi Department of Corrections (and likely many other state governments) grossly underestimate the value of chaplains in the general well being of a prison. People in bondage need hope, and they need to believe in something outside of themselves.

There are indeed many counterfeits to the power of redemption that comes only through Christ, and a lot of well-meaning people try to offer a substitute for the power of Christ to change lives. One supervisor informed me that he was "spiritual, not religious," and I accepted it at face value – until I heard someone in his group session one night counsel the prisoners, saying, *"That light bulb over there could be your Higher Power."* It was then I was reminded that the struggles with the powers of darkness included those with good intentions. Offering a counterfeit to the real, living Spirit of God is as dangerous as leaving them on their own, with no hope.

Though many of the programs in public institutions are based on shallow principles with no spiritual, life-changing power, there were also quite a few which met needs in a very practical way. Until 2012, Mississippi had a Family Visitational program for A-Custody (or Trustee) convicts, which allowed family members to visit their incarcerated loved ones in small apartments. At Parchman, these apartments were located near Camp Three, and we all enjoyed looking out at the children playing in the yard. The mother and father cooked food, that was brought from home, on grills provided by the prison. Programs such as these offered incentives for obeying the rules, as well as benefited the children who suffer greatly from the absence of a parent.

There were staff members outside the Chaplain's office who had a unique talent for effective communication, without fancy counseling degrees, and I learned much from them. Wayne Fleming, a senior staff security officer, was especially gifted in managing troublesome convicts, and was respected by the convict population for his fair and consistent approach and his fun-loving personality.

On one occasion, in the then-new Unit 29 complex, the Emergency Response Team (ERT) was summoned because a convict was threatening a suicide jump from a high tier of his building. The ERT's arrived with sirens blaring and lights flashing. A state of emergency was declared, and all the convicts were locked down. The authoritative commands of the ERT unit for the man to come down were ignored by the terrified man. I was present when Wayne was notified, and he asked me to accompany him. I watched and listened as he quietly said to the convict, *"Now Jerry, come on down here and let's talk about this."* Jerry came down, and I learned a lot about treating prisoners as fellow human beings. Jerry was placed in Protective Custody and I was asked later to pray with him about a serious family situation.

I visited the Maximum Security Unit every week, to share the Scriptures with those who were interested, or to visit with those who just needed a listening ear. Some of these convicts had committed heinous crimes, but I knew that God had not abandoned them. I often cried when I left the misery of that building, because so many would not accept the forgiveness that was so available to them through Christ.

There is much misery and gloom in a prison, but the humorous side of humanity emerged on countless occasions, breaking the tensions and lightening spirits. One Christmas,

I ventured to direct a play starring convicts, and I carefully chose both black and white, male and female, to avoid any show of favoritism. There were dialects ranging from the distinctively black Delta, to the very white Mississippi hills drawl. One of our wise men could only say "*axe*" instead of "*ask*," while my British accent confused him even more by pronouncing it "*ahhsk*." Mary simply could not pronounce "propitiation."

On the day of the performance for the prison staff, the curtains hanging on the makeshift wire with paper clips frequently failed to work properly and had to be dragged open and shut. The cardboard manger suddenly collapsed, and the baby Jesus' arm fell off. The prompter was rather loud, and Joseph's homemade beard was crooked. Back stage, I laughed until I cried. There was surely no Christmas play in the state that year that was more thoroughly enjoyed, both during and after the performance.

Our Bible studies and worship services were attended with anticipation, and visiting speakers often experienced the humor still alive amongst the inmates. A minister conducting a service in one of our camps, concerned that he not exceed his time limit, asked from the podium, *"How much time do I have?"* A convict, not missing a beat, yelled out, *"Well, I don't know about you, Preacher, but I have to go in 20 years."*

The convicts loved to tease me about my misadventures or "goof ups." One day, as I sat catching up on seemingly endless reports, I began to burn and itch, breaking out in red whelps all over my body. At the urgings of my concerned convict helpers, I went to the prison doctor, who diagnosed hives and gave me Benadryl. It relieved the symptoms, but I could barely stand up and my speech became slurred. My youthful convicts were fascinated and gathered around staring. *"Ain't never seen a stoned Chaplain before!"* they exclaimed.

On another occasion, I took one of my helpers with me to tell a fellow convict, Jason, that his brother Clarence had died. Jason was, of course, very upset, and I prayed for him, *"Lord, please comfort Clarence during this time of bereavement."* When we left the building, my helper, Joe, said to me, *"You just prayed for the deceased."* The Lord knew who had died, and I can only hope that He comforted the brother in spite of my absentmindedness. Joe, meanwhile, got much pleasure from telling the story with much embellishment.

I was frequently asked in those beginning years if I feared being a female in such a large and notorious prison. I can honestly say that it never occurred to me to be afraid. I remember standing in the middle of some very brawny, muscular male convicts one day, thoroughly chewing them out for their recent behavior. With bowed heads, they all apologized sheepishly. It wasn't until later that it occurred to me how funny that was. I was only five feet tall and 105 pounds.

I was well aware that many of the men had homemade weapons, referred to on the inside as "shanks." The instruments were made from sharpened spoons, toothbrushes with razor blades in the handles, pieces of sharpened iron from bunk beds and various other items. I saw one such weapon that was fashioned out of razor wire from the very fence that penned them inside of this living hell. I was in the cafeteria one day when a man used his shank on another convict who tried to get ahead of him in the chow line. Most of the men, however, kept their weapons hidden and used them only as protection.

One of my friends marveled at how I almost jumped into her arms one day when a frog leaped out in front of us as we took an evening walk. *"She isn't afraid of rapists and murderers, but she is terrified of a frog,"* she would tell people incredulously. Even the convicts knew of my dislike for things that croak and jump, and one very young prisoner somehow managed to put a frog in the windshield wiper of my car one evening as I prepared to go home. Given my relative fear factor, I suppose that God knew not to send me to the jungles as a missionary. Instead, he sent me further into the confines of prison walls.

Chapter Six

Castle Grayskull

"On Parchman's farm at night,
The moan of prisoners?
Or ghosts?"

From Delta Haikus, © Geoffrey Wilson

A prison within a prison; how much deeper into the depths of confinement could one possibly go? Fifteen hundred male convicts were about to find out.

Castle Grayskull, appropriately nicknamed by its inhabitants, was an immense, sprawling, gray concrete edifice completely surrounded by razor wire and guard towers. This new section of Parchman, officially named Unit 29, was built as a separate entity of the prison, with its own Deputy Warden and staff. Having many years of experience now as a full-time chaplain with BAIC, I was approached about applying for the position of the new State Chaplain for Unit 29. In what I considered to be an act of God, I was hired, and began the task of organizing the brand new Chaplain's department. So began my career as a paid employee of the State of Mississippi, responsible for the spiritual life of the biggest unit in the Mississippi State Penitentiary at Parchman.

The men were not yet in place behind those forbidding walls when two friends from my hometown in England came to visit me. Marlene, Margaret and I walked across the grounds, entering the empty buildings of Castle Grayskull, and asking God to touch the hearts of every man soon to be housed there.

After they left, I sat down on the ground one day, my mind wandering back to the small fishing village in England where my life began. That world seemed so simple and uncomplicated, compared to what my life had become. I reached over and raked my hand through the parched, cracked soil of this Delta land, and felt the centuries of abuse and tragedy.

The seeds of iniquity from both sides – lawmakers and lawbreakers alike – were deeply planted in these soils, springing forth anew each year to yield their harvest. From the Indian burial grounds of the Choctaws, to the aging slave plantation homes, remnants of human abuse were scattered across the state. Nowhere were the wages of sin and death more prevalent than in the very spot where I now sat. I suddenly felt like a poor, untrained field worker who had been given the responsibility for re-seeding an entire plantation. It was as though God had handed me a lone shovel and said, *"DIG."* The task seemed insurmountable. The ground was hard, with twisted roots of bitterness, choked with the weeds of desolation.

God promises that He will not give us responsibility without equipping us with the skills we need to meet it. I spent four exhaustive years at Castle Grayskull, serving as Christ's ambassador from a makeshift office over the prison gym. It had no insulation to prevent the thump-thump-thumping of basketballs from penetrating my walls, a sound which I could sometimes hear in my bed at night as I tried to sleep after 10 or 12 hours at the prison. There was no air-conditioning, and the heat was suffocating in the searing, humid heat of Mississippi's summer months. My reading glasses would slide from my nose, as my hair went from damp to soaked.

I suppose this was as close to suffering as I had ever been in my lifetime, and it was hard sometimes to see the purpose in it all. But God, in His wisdom, knew that the most sincere forms of sympathy are those that come from shared suffering. Though my discomfort was minor in comparison to those who God had brought me to minister to, sharing the same elements of nature and environment brought a legitimacy to my ability to empathize with those around me.

I did not know at the time that this was preparation for something to come and that I would be chosen to head the Chaplain's Department at a brand new state prison facility miles away, which was still years from being built. In those years to come, God would bring forth a thriving, successful ministry from within my department, overflowing with life and energy and transformed lives. The very core of that ministry would come from conversions and programs that had their beginnings right there in Castle Grayskull. The preparations for those years of fruitfulness came from hard experience learned (and earned!) during these years of hardship at Unit 29.

I suppose that the most valuable lesson I learned in that time period, one that would teach me caution and discernment, involved one of the inmates who I had chosen to be my helper. Convicts considered it a good "catch" to be chosen to work for the Chaplain, and many attempted to "get on my hip" (a prison term for getting on my good side). Two of my most valued and trusted inmate brothers, Sheldon Gooch and Joe Elliott, who would later accompany me to the new prison and be the foundation of our convict ministry team, did indeed come from Castle Grayskull. However, as God says in Ecclesiastes, there is a time for sorrow as well as a time for rejoicing. Not all of my helpers would find the freedom available through Christ, inside or outside the prison walls.

One of the first inmates I requested to be my assistant was a young man whose diligence and faithful Christian characteristics I had observed. I felt that I could trust him to represent our department with his fellow convicts. For several years, he did just that. He, along with Sheldon and others, was classified to go with me on speaking trips to churches, schools and other organizations, where they would share their story of conversion. Their deportment was exemplary, and the impact they had on young people was phenomenal. It was a privilege, of course, for the men to be allowed outside the prison gates. They were instrumental in positively influencing hundreds of people, young and old alike, to turn from drugs and crime to become what the Bible calls new creations. The trips were tiring, but fulfilling, and I thank God for the opportunity He gave for these men to help break the cycle of sin and crime in our state.

After several years, this young man became eligible for parole. Having associated with him almost daily, I was convinced that he would not be a threat to society. With genuine conviction and much fervor, I went to the parole board on his behalf. In the words of Moses, I dramatically stretched out my arms and implored, *"Let my people go."* They did!

Two weeks later, he was back in a county jail after violating his parole. I have learned many hard lessons in my life, but this was by far the most difficult and humiliating of them all. I felt that I just could not face the officials at the prison, or the convicts, ever again. After all, it was I who had elevated him to a privileged position in the prison, and it was partly on my own recommendation that he had been released. His failure hurt so many people, and especially it hurt me. My pride was deeply injured; how could I possibly walk back into the prison amidst what I viewed as my own failure? I stayed at home, devastated and crying, until my supervisor (who was not particularly religious) arrived at my house. *"I cannot go back,"* I told him tearfully. He looked me straight in the eyes and said, *"Like hell you can!"* And I did.

The Warden at the time was furious and did not mind telling me so. There was a lot of snickering and more than a few "I told you so's." At the next church service, I spoke of the failures of Abraham and King David, and of the need for taking care, lest we too fail. My faith in my own ability to discern was shaken, but it was a lesson that I needed to learn. I did not become pessimistic, but it did make me very cautious. The Department of Corrections eventually made the decision that staff could no longer make recommendations to the Parole Board. Until that time, however, I did ask that others be considered for release – after much prayer! All of them successfully re-entered society.

Even the weather sometimes matched the oppressive grayness of the concrete structures that held us all inside their walls. At certain times of the year, violent storms occurred, and we were put under tornado watches or warnings. Convicts would be hurriedly returned to their buildings as a Yellow Alert went into effect. Yellow status requires a count of the entire population of the prison in their respective housing units. Staff anxiously scanned the skies, listening to radios as they locked down the units.

One evening, as we enjoyed a particularly relaxed worship service in the gym, an unexpected storm erupted, causing an immediate electrical failure. The lights went out and the doors were locked, waiting for emergency procedures to go into effect. I realized that only a handful of guards and myself were locked in with 300 to 400 convicts, not all of whom had genuinely come to worship! Tension was high, and apprehension could be seen in the faces of many. *"Now what, Lord?"* I asked.

The stillness in the room was eerie, like the silence before a deadly tornado descends upon a population, unleashing its fury. Suddenly I heard the humming begin, and looked up to realize that some of the Christian convicts were swaying from side to side, with their eyes closed, singing softly, then more loudly... *"I'll Fly Away, oh Glory, I'll Fly away. When I die, hallelujah by and by, I'll Fly Away."* This favorite hymn in prisons all over America came to life as everyone joined in. Spirits lifted and everyone, guards and staff and prisoners alike, joined in the fun, with no hint of disturbance whatsoever. The convicts remained until the worst of the storm had passed, as I drove home to the relative safety of my life outside of Parchman.

A level above the Yellow Alert status was the Red Alert, which indicated that either an escape was in progress or that someone could not be located. We were frequently reminded that convicts would try to escape. *"Not from 29,"* I thought. It did, however, happen one night. Through careful planning, some men climbed through the ventilation shaft and over the razor wire fence surrounding the unit. Desperate to flee, they took their blankets to cover the deadly wire, but were nonetheless lacerated. Having lost too much blood, one was caught shortly after the alarm sounded. The others were apprehended before they could complete the miles to the main road. They were quickly placed in isolation cells, and the word spread quickly throughout the prison. The usual punishment for attempting to escape is an additional five year sentence and a lengthy spell in protective custody.

Escape attempts were rarely attempted and almost never successful. I was around for another dash towards freedom, where the recaptured convict, in handcuffs and chains, was paraded around the perimeter fence after his capture. After an alligator was pulled out of the swamps near the prison, it too was prominently displayed, reinforcing the message: *Don't even try to leave – it's not worth the risk.*

Weekend duty was a particular challenge, as the Chaplains from all the units rotated responsibility for emergency situations from Friday night until Monday morning. One Chaplain would stay on the grounds of the prison during the entire weekend, and it was rare when an incident of some kind didn't occur. More often than I care to recall, I had the heart-wrenching job of notifying a convict that a family member had died. One evening, I received a call informing us that the twin children of a convict were killed in an accident as they were returning home from visiting their father in prison. There is no good way to deliver the most tragic of news that a parent could ever hear. I spent hours praying and trying to console but, in that situation, there was not even a practical means of relieving the pain, because the convict was allowed only a telephone call. The women were particularly difficult to bring bad news to, as they would react much more emotionally. After one girl took off running and had to be chased by the guards, and another repeatedly banged her head against the closest wall, I resorted to taking with me security personnel capable of subduing them.

On other occasions, the chaplain would be responsible for notifying family members of a convict's death. In the beginning, I would deliver the news over the telephone, unless it was a local family. After hearing people scream and drop the phone, I eventually began calling the sheriff or police station to make the initial contact, making myself available afterwards for questions or prayer. Sleep did not come easily after such close encounters with tragedy.

Before my ministry at the prison began, I had been involved in a movement known as the Lay Witness Missions. Ordinary people from churches all over America would join together and spend a weekend at a particular church, sharing what God had done in their lives. I had an idea to hold a Lay Witness Mission at the prison one weekend, but organization proved to be a nightmare.

Housing, food and transportation for dozens of volunteers in such an isolated place as Parchman required all my ingenuity and strength. The security involved in getting all these people into so many separate camps, including Maximum Security, was phenomenal. It rained the entire weekend, causing many of the roads to become a mud bath, with entry into the secured buildings creating a hazard for the visitors.

The stress of this mammoth undertaking became evident when I attempted to get out of bed on Sunday morning. The pain in my back was so intense that I could not move. I was staying in the guest house on the prison grounds, so I had to wait until a convict was sent to announce breakfast before I could notify anyone about my condition. I was given some powerful pain medication, and the prison ambulance arrived with much fanfare. I was loaded onto a stretcher, only to discover that it could not be maneuvered around the corridors of the guest house. Convict ingenuity prevailed, and I was hauled out through the window! There was cheering as the ambulance, with lights flashing and sirens blaring, left for the hospital in my home town of Cleveland, Mississippi. The Lay Witness Mission went on without me and was a triumph of the Lord. In spite of all the problems, it was repeated in future years.

Other weekends were decidedly more relaxed and carefree. A favorite event, with both the prisoners and the surrounding townspeople, was when the visiting rodeos unleashed their energy onto the grounds. In those years, the convicts were allowed to participate in some of the activities, including retrieving money from the head of a bull. It was dangerous, but our macho men enjoyed the challenge, the notoriety and the monetary prizes. On the day it was performed for convicts, a female prisoner would be chosen as the rodeo's Beauty Queen, amidst much whistling and cheering from the men.

It was my job at the rodeo to bring the invocation; how does one pray at a rodeo? I usually just said something like,

"Thank you, Lord, for being with us and for allowing us time of recreation." What I was really thinking was, *"Please don't let the bull get them!"*

It now occurs to me that a rodeo in a prison is not your everyday occurrence. It was not planned primarily for the entertainment of the convicts, but with so much acreage available, the prison was the ideal place to hold the annual event in our area. I think that convict participation was part of the interest from the local populace, who flocked to the event. Much has changed over the years, and the rodeo is no longer held at Parchman. As the prison population grew, it no doubt became a security nightmare.

As the years went by, my four children, John, Wendy Leigh, Glynis and Bill, grew up and moved on with their lives. When the grandchildren started arriving, I realized that if I was going to spend any time with them at all, I would have to involve them in my prison activities. I could rarely take time off from work when my first grandchild came to visit, and so I would bring her into Unit 29 with me, where she played happily in my office with my inmate helpers. She was particularly enamored with Joe Elliott, who was so kind and fun with her. I watched one day as he and another convict pulled Tiffany (the first grandchild) around in a large box, which they called a car. Though she is grown now and became a lawyer herself after graduating from Ole Miss law school, she still fondly remembers the days she spent in prison as a child.

Most of my other grandchildren after that spent time behind bars (in a manner of speaking). When I worked with inmate women in the new prison, my helpers were thrilled to be able to play with young children again, as Jessica, Kayte, Read and Emily took turns visiting on their summer vacations. My grandson, Brantley, visited from his home in California for Thanksgiving one year and was shocked to find that our family gathering included prisoners and that dinner was to be held in our prison chapel, surrounded by razor wire and armed guards. My grandchildren will probably always remember bragging to their friends about "being in prison"; I suppose that few children could top *those* stories! My youngest grandchild, Kelly Leigh, was not yet born during my days in prison, but she still knows many of my convict "children" in their after-incarceration free lives.

Overall, I found the life of a prison chaplain in those years to be one of long hours, dealing with multitudes of people with little or no choices left in their lives. I saw firsthand that there is no truth in the non-Biblical saying "God only helps those who help themselves." If that were the case, then an entire segment of our society, those behind bars, would be abandoned by Him and left with no hope. In the early days of my chaplaincy, the convicts did not even have telephone privileges unless a chaplain verified an emergency and remained to monitor the call. These were people who no longer had the ability to help themselves.

The needs were constant, with a myriad of problems, ranging from family concerns to spiritual matters. The chaplains were the only help convicts had in these situations. Who was going to care if marriages fell apart or children strayed? Who else was going to hold their hands and pray with them? Who else was going to be concerned about their eternal destiny which, after all, comes to each of us?

Chapter Seven

Women's Maximum Security

Central Mississippi Correctional Facility

Human bondage, whatever form it takes, is not easy to look upon. Although I understood the necessity of iron restraints on the legs and arms of newly arrived convicts, it was always unsettling to watch them bound and shuffling in their yellow jumpsuits. Each time I entered either the

Reception Center or Maximum Security and saw a face peeking out at me through narrow window slits in the door, I was reminded of animals in a cage. The sounds they made often sounded like animals, too, as they called out *"I need to talk to you,"* or pleaded, *"Help Me."* Knowing that those in Maximum Security spent 23 hours a day in 6x9 foot cells, with nothing to do, made my heart ache to reach out to them with the news that there is hope in Jesus. With thousands of inmates in my care, though, and each one a tragedy of their own making, the ability and time to care for them all simply was not there.

A chaplain may enter any area in the prison, so I visited all buildings at least once a week, including Women's Maximum Security. Those incarcerated in "Max" included women with long sentences who had recently arrived from county jails, those with serious rules violations (fighting or attacking an officer, etc.), some with mental problems, potential suicides, and those on Death Row.

Standing at the metal door to Maximum Security, I would brace myself for the inevitable sounds of women screaming. They yelled to one another or to the guards, pushing their emergency buttons in desperate but often ignored attempts to get attention. After waiting to hear the "click" of the lock as it was released for me, I would push that heavy door and enter an entirely different world.

In the summer months, the building felt like a furnace. A narrow, barred window in each cell opened from the inside to let in some air, but with temperatures sometimes reaching 100 degrees, the heat was suffocating. In the winter, the poorly designed heating system made the building just as unbearably hot. Some were allowed to have fans, if provided by their families, and the chaplain's department arranged donated ones for those who could not afford it. Stirring up hot air, however, is less than a relief, and it often reminded me of my early days in Mississippi, before the luxury of air-conditioned homes.

Having been around for so many years now, most of the guards knew me, and I rarely had to present ID as I entered the Maximum Security building. Some officers considered me a nuisance and resented my presence in their closely guarded domain. One of their favorite ways of showing it was to "forget" to open doors to cells I had requested to enter, or to delay in releasing the girls for our church services. Other guards, however, realized that I was there to help, and would refer individuals to me, "Chaplain, the new girl with a life sentence in cell 210 is not eating" or "How about checking on Nancy in the suicide cell?" Those attempting suicide would be clothed in paper gowns in a cell with only a mattress, anything dangerous to them having been removed. Many times I found myself sitting on the concrete floor of a cramped cell, praying with a woman curled up in a fetal position, having lost all hope.

The women were allowed out of their cells for only an hour each day, time enough for a quick shower and 45 minutes of yard time (in either an outdoor pen or the day area inside). With the exception of Death Row inmates, who were allowed no contact with others, this time outside was the women's only chance to be together. When I conducted church services, I was well aware that many of them came into the day area just for the contact with other human beings, but I encouraged their attendance regardless of their motives.

Our church services were routinely interrupted by inmates who did not attend, as they beat on their doors or screamed for the guards, sometimes out of sheer frustration. *"Girls, continue to sing while I talk to Jenny or Latisha,"* I would say. Sometimes the only way to create calm was to humble them into quietness by reminding them that we were trying to worship the Lord. Peace would reign for a few moments, only to be displaced by agitation over and over again.

Women like Clara, who had killed her own baby in a particularly heinous manner, were seized with uncontrollable anger most of the time. For years, Clara remained trapped in the dual prison of her steel cage and her own mind. In lucid moments, a smile would break through as I stopped by her cell, giving me a glimpse of the woman she must have once been. In those rare times, she would voice her concerns, even allowing me to pray with her very briefly. My real ministry to Clara, however, was in the prayers I uttered for her in the privacy of my own home.

There were very few people I could tell about my struggles with what I considered "powers of darkness." Not all Christian believers understand the war that rages between God and the devil or the activities of evil spirits. I would no doubt have been classified insane myself if I had tried to explain the occasional presence of evil spirits in and amongst my women prisoners. I sometimes found it necessary to invoke the name of Jesus, as instructed in the Bible, when I believed the verbal attacks on me were demonic. After hearing a guttural male voice emanating one day from a slight, frail female, I spoke to it directly, *"In the name of Jesus, come out of her."* After a bellow, she returned to a normal state of mind and body. She later became a believer in Christ and is today out of prison; by all accounts, she is functioning well in her freedom.

Margaret was plagued by mental apparitions, constantly terrified by the "heads" she saw floating in her cell. *"When that happens,"* I suggested, *"call out to Jesus."* One day she stopped me and announced triumphantly, *"I did what you told me – the heads are gone!"* The Bible says that our war is not against flesh and blood, but against powers and principalities. They are not even always so easy to differentiate. One woman in another camp at the prison always disrupted the worship services when she was (to use her own words) "in the Spirit." Others believed her to be truly touched by God when she ran up and down the aisles, falling on the floor as she was "slain in the Spirit." However, I sensed a spirit other than that of the true and living God. One day, I simply had enough of it all, and sent the other girls back to their seats. I leaned over to her and gently whispered, *"In the name of Jesus, get out of her."* She immediately sat up and calmly walked back to her seat, never to disrupt again.

During my years as a chaplain to these women, I worked with some on Death Row, who were awaiting execution. Several stayed there for years before appeals granted them a sentence reduction, and eventual release into the general population of the prison. Those on Death Row were not allowed to associate with other convicts, and family members could visit only twice a month. Yet they could see a chaplain, and so my Bible studies were almost always welcomed. Though some embraced them only as a respite from the monotony of their isolated cells, others did show genuine interest. They spent so many years in these conditions that I would leave wondering how they retained their sanity. Not all of them did.

Jane was convicted and received a death sentence for conspiring to kill a relative. She always maintained that she was innocent, and that her husband was the guilty party. He had indeed been convicted as well, but only received a life sentence. Jane claimed that a lot of money had exchanged hands to prevent him from getting the death penalty that had been doled out to her. My job was never one that included the determination of guilt or innocence, though I will say that I did think it odd that her husband served his time in the county jail, rather than in a state prison.

For several years, Jane handled her strict confinement extraordinarily well. She enjoyed my visits, and thrived on our times of prayer and Bible study, smothering me in hugs when I arrived or departed. She became engrossed in the craft of embroidery, which I was able to provide for her from the gifts of kind donors. At one point, we even managed to acquire a television set for her. Her hearing and sight were very poor, but the Department of Corrections eventually provided glasses and a hearing aid for her. The chaplain's department replaced the batteries for the hearing aid when necessary, which was often, as she somehow managed to lose them even in a 6x9 foot cell.

Her children visited twice a month for an hour or two, and she relished the mail that she was allowed to receive. Though regulations dictated that Jane be allowed outside in a fenced pen for about an hour each day, I had to fight for this right on her behalf more than once. She would routinely be given her hour inside the day room, with no access to fresh air.

I considered it a good sign that she remained concerned with her appearance, keeping her uniforms neat and using cosmetics which she received from home. Her earrings would match the occasional red bow and mandatory red jumpsuit, that highlighted her brilliant, auburn hair.

Though it was strictly forbidden, the hair was obviously dyed, and no doubt most officials thought I was her "source" for the relatively harmless contraband hair supplies. In actuality, the lady who aided her in this venture, though well-meaning, could easily have lost her job for this ill-advised act of kindness.

Jane never did understand my unwillingness to break the rules in matters like this. I suppose that, when locked in a tiny metal "cage" day in and day out, your world becomes very small and it is difficult to see beyond your immediate needs. The smallest things take on inflated significance, and your own predicament is all that you can see.

Jane's downward spiral began when the privilege of working with handcrafts was eliminated for all convicts, and she lost her precious needle-works. There was now very little for her to do with the endless days and nights and, as most people in Maximum Security cells, she began to sleep a lot. Then suddenly, her worst fears were realized.

I left to go on vacation and returned to find that they were making preparations for Jane's execution. One of the officials had to ask her the ominous question – *would you prefer the gas chamber or lethal injection?* She was distraught that no prior notice had been given to her, and I reluctantly decided to contact her attorney. I was always unsure of how much I should get involved in the legal aspect of the prisoners lives, as my calling was to administer spiritual comfort and point them towards the One who could truly give them the peace they so desperately needed. In this instance, however, it turned out to be the right thing to do, as her attorney was not even aware of the sudden acceleration of her execution. Subsequently, he intervened and the date was postponed, much to her relief. She had requested that I be present in her final moments, and I must admit that my own relief was measurable as well.

Though her life was spared for the time being, I think that the trauma of it all was just too much for Jane. Her behavior began to change. On some occasions, she would speak to me, and on others there was no response whatsoever. Several times she told me, "*I'm going to marry a movie star,*" or "*My lawyer says I will be out of here tomorrow.*" She constantly misplaced or broke her false teeth, and her weight plummeted. Her spectacles were constantly broken, and her hearing aid either disappeared or she stopped using it. Even when I shouted, she could not hear my words as I strove to communicate with her. I resorted to writing with very large letters on a notepad. She no longer read her Bible or prayed, and I wondered sometimes if she even really knew who I was anymore.

Jane's family was grief-stricken over the change in her, and their visits became less and less frequent. I doubt that she noticed, however. She became unkempt, and her cell was dirty and cluttered. Other convicts were assigned to keep her cell clean, but she viciously accused them of stealing her zoo-zoos and wham-whams (prison slang for edible items purchased from the canteen).

In the end, all that I could do for Jane was to periodically determine if she was being treated fairly. She was transferred to a county jail to await a new trial and finally died there. It is with deep sadness that I reflect on the many years of her life spent in the misery of a Death Row cell, and then in the confusion of her own mind. I do believe, however, that she is now with her Lord. She will never live in confinement again – and Jesus has taken her into His loving arms.

"Free at last, Free at last,
I thank God I'm free at last.
Way down yonder in the graveyard walk,
I thank God I'm free at last.
Me and my Jesus gonna meet and talk,
I thank God I'm free at last."

(*American Negro Songs* by J.W. Work)

Chapter Eight

Lil' Bits of Love

"I can do no great thing,
Only small things with great love."

Mother Theresa

Late one night, a freckle-faced, sandy-haired child evangelist from Australia descended the steps of a Greyhound bus, and walked into the intense heat and mosquitoes of a Mississippi Delta summer. I picked up

Stephen Reinmuth in my car and drove him toward the "mission," for which he had crossed continents.

Stephen entered a world that he had never seen before, not knowing a soul and possessing only what he deemed a calling from God. He came for one reason alone: to minister God's love to a criminal whose own mother was quoted in a magazine article as saying, *"Send my son to the gas chamber."*

Stephen was here to visit Jimmy Lee Gray, a convicted murderer with a death sentence for the brutal slaying of a young child. Stephen had read about Jimmie Lee in the publication that quoted his mother, and he was shocked by the statement. He was prompted by God to write Jimmy Lee, telling him that even such a horrid crime was forgivable through Jesus Christ.

After more than a year of correspondence, both Stephen and Jimmy Lee were convinced that God wanted him to come to Mississippi. How could this young pastry chef from Australia get enough money for such an expensive trip? As time went by, even those who prayed and believed with him began to doubt that he was indeed hearing from God. One day, however, a check for $1000 arrived in the mail. By the following weekend, the entire amount needed for his airfare to America had been supplied.

Stephen boarded a plane headed for Los Angeles, with very little cash, a small suitcase and a guitar. When he walked off the plane hours later, he was in America, but still very far from the farmlands of Mississippi. What now? He spent the night in a motel, praying that God would send someone to guide him in the right path. The next morning, he shared his story with the maid from the hotel, who agreed with him that he could not continue staying in an expensive hotel. *"Come home with me,"* she said. *"Meet my family, and remain with us until you are ready to go to Mississippi."*

A week later, he boarded a plane for Jackson, Mississippi, getting closer to his destination, but still unsure how he would enter the prison grounds. Though Stephen didn't know it at the time, Jimmy Lee was actually en route to Parchman from a county jail, being transferred to begin his wait on Death Row. Stephen again checked into a motel and prayed for God's direction. He awoke the next morning and discovered a Sunday church service in progress at the Methodist church across the street. He (by chance?) was introduced to Morris Thigpen, who was then the Deputy Commissioner of Corrections for the state. Stephen was directed by Morris to none other than Glenn Howell, the former chaplain at Parchman who gave me my first job there as his assistant. Glenn was now the administrator of the Pascagoula Restitution Center on the coast, where Jimmy Lee Gray had been in jail. Glen invited Stephen to stay in his home for a few days and shared his story with the men in the Restitution Center there, before contacting me with the news that Stephen would be heading my way. Stephen had now been passed full circle around the state through the hands of God's people, and was finally to be delivered into my care for the fulfillment of his mission to visit Jimmy Lee.

By a miracle of God, Chaplain Padgett and other prison officials arranged for Stephen to spend time with Jimmy Lee in his Maximum Security building for two days a week. Upon finally meeting, the two men embraced and began a friendship that would continue until the end. Jimmy Lee had repented and dedicated his life to Christ by then, so they prayed and talked and sang together. They laughed and they cried, growing strong in their commitment to Christ and to one another.

Stephen also ministered life and hope to others at the prison, spending hours sharing the Good News in various camps at the penitentiary. He accompanied me to the county jail every Sunday, much to the delight of the men incarcerated there, who had never met an Australian. They listened attentively to every word this odd sounding fellow said, commenting, "He's even harder to understand than YOU, Mrs. Wendy!" I suppose my British English was still very evident in the land of Southern drawls, though my family in England considered my accent very changed. On one of my trips home, my father just shook his head at my new Southern way of talking. "My dear, whatever has happened to your speech?" My only defense was, "I can't help it, Daddy. I'm surrounded by them!"

Stephen stayed with us until the very emotional day when Jimmie Lee was baptized in the prison chapel. Soon afterwards, Stephen returned to Australia, having made an enormous impact on the lives of countless people in this Delta land so far from his home of birth. He continued his correspondence and friendship with Jimmy Lee from afar.

Jimmy Lee Gray went to the gas chamber silently on September 2, 1983, the first execution in Mississippi since the death penalty was reinstated after a Supreme Court ruling in 1976. Less than a year later, the state switched to lethal injection, outlawing the gas chamber, partially due to what was considered a botched execution when Jimmy Lee endured prolonged suffering in the last moments of his life. Mississippi's gas chamber was completely decommissioned in 1998.

Hating the fascination that people had for his crime, Jimmy Lee had refused to speak publicly about his conversion. He had no desire to be perceived as one who would use the name of Jesus to escape punishment. He understood that he had to pay for his earthly crime. As a mother myself, I cannot imagine the victim's family ever offering forgiveness for the horrendous act he committed, but Jimmy Lee ultimately went to his death forgiven by a Savior whose love surpasses all understanding. He was ready to meet his Lord.

I will never forget this young man from Australia who I had fondly nicknamed "Lil Bit." Hebrews 13:2 says to take care, as we may sometimes be entertaining angels unaware. As a woman who has spent her life with hardened criminals, discerning intentions and motives and hearts, it takes a lot to surprise me – and I wouldn't have been at all taken aback to one day learn that my "Lil' Bit" was a messenger from farther away than Australia! I did, however, many years later, receive a musical CD in the mail from a much older Stephen Reinmuth, still alive and on God's earth, many miles from Mississippi.

Though Stephen Reinmuth came the farthest distance to share God's love to those in bondage, there were countless others who gave of their time and talents. Spanning the years from Camp Three to Castle Grayskull to my new position as Head Chaplain at the new prison built near the state's capital, they came steadily as God tugged at their heart strings.

There was no "typical" volunteer who stepped in to minister inside the prison walls. From the gentle-spirited to the vivacious, young or old, male and female alike, they came. One of the first regular volunteers at Parchman's Unit 29, was a retired missionary in his seventies. White-haired and slightly stooped with age, George Stewart would shuffle through the buildings with his bag of literature. At lunchtime, he would nap in a plastic chaise lounge in our office space above the gym, oblivious to the incessant noise below which so plagued my own senses. He was loved by the convicts, who eagerly awaited his gentle spirit and kind ways.

Well into her eighties, a vivacious Joyce Horton came to the prison for many years, teaching Bible studies and counseling female convicts. When her health began to fail, her husband Frank drove her to the prison, waiting patiently until she finished. She continued bringing life into the prison as long as her own continued.

If some enter with the gentleness of a dove, others roar with the voice of lions. Kent Bergeron, with his group of Christian motorcyclists, zoomed in to the prison one day during an evangelistic crusade – and never really went away! When they first arrived, clad in leather and bandanas, long hair flying, I received a call from a concerned security officer. *"Are you SURE these guys are approved?"* he asked. They related so powerfully to the men that I invited them to come twice a month, and they continued coming for several years.

Another group of motorcyclists, some formerly Hells Angels, came one day, along with a Nascar driver, all of them roaring around the grounds. It totally amazed me that the convicts were allowed to ride behind them, even the squealing females. On one occasion, the Warden himself rode his four-wheeler with them, as I hung on the back for dear life, to the cheering of delighted onlookers. Well-known evangelistic teams like Bill Glass came occasionally, bringing celebrity entertainers and athletes.

Among the favorite volunteers in prisons are ex-offenders, who return to offer hope for a life after imprisonment. Kenny Williams, a former drug addict and armed robber, started his own prison ministry called *Captives Set Free*. During his long imprisonment, his professional singing voice and amazing ability to articulate his faith made him a true asset to our own prison speaking team, *Captives for Christ*. We did, however, have to insist that he wear long-sleeved shirts to cover the partially nude female tattooed on his arm. *"Kenny, people will not be listening to what you have to say if they are looking at your lady,"* I explained. On hot days, he would grumble and I would have to remind him that long-sleeved shirts were but another consequence of poor past decisions. I can still close my eyes and envision this large young man in his striped prison uniform, bringing tears to the eyes of convicts and "free worlders" alike, singing *"The old man is dead."*

On equal footing with power is the calm voice of grace. Arriving with shimmering scenery and exquisite costumes, Ballet Magnificat glided onto the stage of our prison life. A Christian classical ballet company based in Jackson, they pulled up to the gym on the first of many times that they performed for us. Some of the male convicts were assigned to help them unload and set up their equipment. The male dancers, dressed in blue jeans and tennis shoes, assisted in the unloading, laughing and joking with the convicts. After a while, the dancers began to do their warm-up exercises and, much to the astonishment of the convicts, their blue-jean clad new buddies began to leap and twirl. To the open-mouthed inmates, the dancers turned around and said, *"yep, we're the ballet dudes."* The wildly cheering convict audience at their performance, both that night and on many more to come, was enthusiastic in embracing a cultural event that was foreign to most all of them.

"Even Cicadas stop singing
To hear a gospel choir in the country"
© Geoffrey Wilson, Delta Haikus

On one Saturday each summer, the choruses of a multitude of gospel choirs could be heard for miles around the prison gates. Like Gabriel's army of angels, visiting church choirs descended upon the "yards" for our annual Music Festival. The atmosphere of the prison was temporarily transformed into one not unlike a church "picnic on the grounds."

In all the years that we held this festival, it never once rained and no incident ever sprang forth from within or without. We were allowed to sell hot dogs and cakes, with the proceeds benefiting the Chapel fund for ministry. Volunteers provided funds for those who could not afford the "real, free-world hot dogs," and even Maximum Security convicts were allowed to buy a "goodie." Excluded from physical participation in this, or any other event, they could still hear the music floating through the air and penetrating walls, chains and fences.

Dozens of volunteers worked hard to make this day a special one for our guys and girls, and I am still thankful to them. Some of the senior officials at the prison, as well as security personnel, even came in on their day off to ensure adequate protection for everyone involved.

Though special events were an enormous release for the stress and building tensions of everyday life in prison, it is the day-to-day sacrifices of individuals like Ben Malone that no doubt have the most lasting effects in changing lives. Ben began working as a volunteer in the Reception Center where prisoners were first introduced to their new "home." He began adding more and more days each week to his schedule at the prison, and eventually came to the conclusion that the Lord wanted him to sell his business and become a full-time volunteer chaplain. In his late 40's, this dedicated servant of Christ was approved by the Department of Corrections to work beside me on a daily basis, at his own expense. I wasn't alone anymore! He even stayed at the prison during the week, in a small apartment attached to our newly built chapel, until the authorities deemed it a security risk.

Ben is remembered by thousands and thousands of prisoners as the "man with the hats" for the bright, sometimes outrageous hats he wore to match his sunny personality. He was also known as the prison Santa Claus for his role in delivering gift boxes of personal hygiene items, candy and socks, etc. to the convicts each Christmas.

Provided by local church groups, I delivered these boxes myself for many years, before dashing off to visit my own children. Volunteers came for the annual Christmas party, complete with food, games and singing. This tradition, which began in my first year at the new prison in Central Mississippi, was a real challenge to accomplish as the number of inmates increased dramatically. The Christmas before I retired, the Warden had carts painted red to carry the boxes, and he accompanied our Santa as he delivered them to over 3,000 convicts.

This particular Warden was different, but kind, and he understood the depression of convicts separated from their loved ones during the holidays. He wisely participated in this morale booster to alleviate the potential for problems within the prison as the world on the outside celebrated freedom, in both religious and traditional ways.

Entertaining convicts? *Aren't we supposed to be punishing them?* I have often been asked this by those shortsighted enough to miss the "bigger picture."

Paying the consequences for crime is necessary if people are to live together in a society. But most of these men and women, when released, will return to a life on the streets, with poverty and crime beckoning them at every turn. Perhaps showing them how to find pleasure in small ways, like singing and praying and celebrating God's goodness, will give them a glimpse of a life where enjoyment need not involve drugs, immorality or crime. An occasional day spent away from the monotony and tension of normal prison life, with people outside of their own circles, perhaps reminds them of the humanity that will one day be restored to them when they return to society. It is sometimes the simple things that contribute most to broadening their view of what the world could be for them.

There are countless others who have left their mark in the world of "inside ministry." My friend Helen once pointed out that *"anyone who is a friend of Wendy's usually ends up in prison."* Dennis Royall, a music professor at Delta State University, was an answer to prayer in many ways, joining in reaching out to those in the County jail, as well as at Parchman. His wife, Dorothy, laughed one day as I hurriedly jumped out of a small airplane piloted by Dennis. His good intentions of flying me to our speaking engagement so that I could be more rested were countered by high winds, and my heart was racing by the time I turned to them both and said emphatically, *"Thank you and God Bless You – but I will NEVER do that again!"*

A particularly unique ministry out of Washington D.C. became involved at Parchman through their contact with our famous ex-KKK prisoner Tommy Tarrants. Headed by the equally newsworthy Chuck Colson, former aide to President Nixon, indicted and charged in the Watergate scandal, Prison Fellowship issued an invitation for Tommy to attend one of their seminars in Washington. The governor granted special permission, and Tommy was issued "free world" clothing and sent to this historic event.

The friendship that developed between Chuck and Tommy resulted in a chapter of Prison Fellowship being founded in Mississippi. Chuck Colson came personally to share his story with our men and women, many of whom had read his autobiography *"Born Again."* As I met this man and his entourage at the front gate of the prison, I was struck first by his full stature as he towered over me. But his warmth and humility immediately surpassed his overpowering presence, which he used so effectively in impacting the convicts with the power of God to transform.

Exceedingly articulate and educated, Chuck Colson showed little desire for personal recognition as he communicated easily and comfortably with the predominantly uneducated population of the prison. Many years later, we were to meet again by chance at a church in England. Miles away from the prisons of America, our common bonds nonetheless drew us together as he grabbed me in a huge bear hug, remembering me as the little Chaplain in a great big world of thieves and murderers. His ministry in our country's jails and prisons continued until his death in 2012, and Prison Fellowship is still active in all 50 states to this day.

There are no words to adequately describe the impact of Stuart Irby, Jr., a man with extraordinary insight and ingenuity. This renowned businessman and philanthropist, who contributed so much financially to programs which encouraged spiritual outcomes, also stood out for his ability to understand what many of our state leaders do not: the need for deep spiritual experiences along with academic achievement.

Stuart sponsored several essay contests among the convicts, designed to make them think. The winners were honored at a banquet with exquisite food, bouquets of flowers for the ladies, and entertainment for everyone. Rewarded for an intellectual pursuit, most of them for the first time in their lives, they were given certificates and generous monetary awards. The cash was placed into accounts to be used as policy allowed, some saving it until their parole and others sending it home to their families.

Volunteers are often misunderstood, their motives questioned, and their presence merely tolerated. People like Dan Williams, who traveled 600 miles each month for years to counsel at the prison on weekends, was not always appreciated by security personnel, who were bothered with having to unlock doors and monitor the prisoners while in his presence. As with most who persevere, however, he was eventually accepted as one who makes their job easier for them in the long run.

Not all had motives as sincere as his, and in fact there are some volunteer organizations which I considered detrimental to the spiritual development of our prisoners. Some came for the personal glory, joining what was considered for a time to be the fashionable ministry at churches. Others came to push their own denominational doctrines, sometimes teaching that salvation was only available to those who belonged to their particular church.

The confusion and quarrelling caused by such groups was disturbing to the convicts, that I perceived to be a security threat for the prison. I often had to fight to prevent these groups from infiltrating the camps, and more than once was threatened and shouted at. I once even put my job on the line as I refused admittance to a group whom I believed to be destructive. Even when they appealed to the Governor's office, I stood my ground, expecting to be fired. God intervened, however, and I returned to my daily chores of administering the truth to those in my care.

Chapter Nine

The Upstairs People

My four children and I lived in a large, old two-story home with a constant flow of their friends bringing enthusiasm, volume and laughter, most of the time. I don't remember making a conscious decision to also invite others to live there, but, as my daughter recently reminded me, there were always people upstairs, some we didn't know. *"We never really knew who would be there when we got home from school,"* she says.

One of our house guests, thinking of a local boarding house, nicknamed it "Ma Hatcher's Boarding House," and the name "Ma" became mine from that point on. Even the convicts adopted that title after hearing a volunteer address me as such, although not in earshot of security personnel. There was never a charge involved at Ma Hatcher's Boarding House, and entrance was gained only by need.

Several college students were "upstairs people" at different times. One young man, Chris Huff, was a strong Christian leader on campus, so our home became the meeting place for groups of praying college Christians. It was a special blessing for me to have these dedicated young people praying for my needs, often getting involved on a practical level.

A group of them appeared one weekend to paint the house, with the only payment being a hamburger meal halfway through. God's helpers swarmed like bees over that house, singing and laughing and splattering paint everywhere.

Chris graduated from Delta State and later received a Master's degree in counseling from Mississippi College. He is now a dedicated counselor for traumatized and abused children.

Billy and Debbie Dempsey joined the upstairs people because there was no room at the married student's living quarters at the university. The first time I met Billy, several years earlier, he was a 15-year-old attending a Christian retreat. I can still see him walking among the trees with a green beanie upon his head and large Bible in his hands. I was a new Christian myself, under some persecution because of my "fanatical" love for Jesus. What an encouragement it was for me to see a young person with such bold dedication.

Billy graduated from Delta State and later Reformed Theological Seminary, to become first a campus minister and later a pastor in a church. The Dempseys now have grown children of their own and I wonder if they remember living with mine and being Upstairs People. With a couple of my teenagers still at home, it must have been a challenge for them!

On other occasions, the outcomes of taking in strangers, and encouraging others to do so, proved devastating. I can't begin to describe the heartbreak and humiliation of having a couple of them arrested, and the personal hurt when one stole my silverware. I haven't always seen God's hand in the apparent failures. There was definitely an element of "self" involved on some occasions.

At one point, a "ministry team" who came to the prison monthly needed somewhere to stay during their weekend visits, so I offered to accommodate them. They came for several months and we had a pleasant enough relationship, although I must admit my friends were somewhat dubious. During this time my father passed away, and I had to make a hurried trip to England. I told the guys they could go ahead and stay for their usual weekend. My now adult children went with me. When I returned I found, to my horror, that this ministry team had used my home for parties and stolen several items, including my son's antique gun collection. The house was filthy, covered with cigarettes and dirty dishes. In addition to all this, I began to hear that they had used my name to solicit money for their "ministry." They had disappeared by that time, of course. After I reported all this to my next-door neighbor, Sheriff Grimmett, he found them in another state and they were promptly jailed. We never regained the stolen items.

I received sad letters from these men reminding me that I was a Christian and should forgive. I did, but the law did not – and rightly so. Their sin was against the God they professed to serve. We often reap the consequences of our actions in order to bring us to repentance. Did they repent? I never heard from them again.

Of course, there are delightful memories as well. One young lady, Anna Jean, came into my life and into our home when her husband had their marriage annulled after finding someone else. I will never forget the outrage when I first heard her story. I let the so-called "Christian" church know what the Bible said about such a decision to allow an annulment, but received no response. She became a follower of Jesus during this period, and her time with us proved to be one of mutual benefit. Our friendship has remained steadfast all these years, as has her commitment to her Lord.

For the sake of my children, and later because it was against Mississippi Department of Corrections policy, I did not invite ex-convicts to be "Upstairs People." There was one guy, however, who was borderline.

As a teenager, "Bubba" Rogers was well-known in the area, most often seen with bare feet, ragged blue jeans, and long untidy hair (before either were fashionable or acceptable.) I didn't really believe everything I had heard about him when I took him in. He was certainly charming when it suited him, with a good sense of humor and an infectious laugh. His potential for a "successful" life was apparent beneath the manipulative style he had adopted. I remember friends telling me, "Wendy, he is using you," to which I usually replied, "yes, I know." I actually cared for him as one of my own – and my own had moments when they tried me too! There were times when I despaired of reaching him, especially when I discovered his involvement with drugs, but I always believed God had a plan for his life.

My friend, Ann Woods, often laughs when we talk about those days. Ann had a Bible study for troubled youth – and they actually came! One evening Bubba, smelling of marijuana, crashed into the glass den door, thinking it was open. It wasn't so funny then, but Ann always handled surprise situations well.

Bubba says of himself, *"Both my parents, while making a public profession of faith, were not active in church. I did attend church with my godly grandmother until her death when I was 14 years old. My grandmother's death was the most significant turning point in my life. At this point, I began to use drugs, smoke, drink and the other things that a 15-year-old teenager does when there are no restrictions placed on him. My high school years were so blurry that even now I cannot recall all the things that happened. I know I left home on more than one occasion and stayed with other families. My senior year was filled with complete disrespect for all authority figures, and due to the increase in my use of drugs, I was unable to do anything that would be considered productive."*

"Soon I was arrested for the sale of amphetamines and sentenced to two years in the State Penitentiary. My life was total chaos and confusion. All the time during my trial date and time of sentencing, the lady who would become my 'Mama Hatcher' would take me into her home and in many ways do things that a mother would do for their very own. I must confess that my heart swells up inside of me as I remember her showing me Jesus' love."

Bubba was sentenced to two years at Parchman Penitentiary, but his sentence was reduced to one year and nine months probation, with three months in a state mental hospital. There was no doubt that God had mercy on this young man's life.

After completing his time in the hospital, he went to Jackson, joining my daughter who went to college there. It was in Jackson that he finally surrendered his life to Jesus. What a change! Shortly after his conversion, he enrolled in Belhaven College and completed his B.A. degree in humanities. From there he went to Georgia State University and completed his M. Ed degree, and eight years later a M. Div. degree from New Orleans Baptist Seminary.

How astounded the whole town was (and still is) upon meeting the new Bubba, who now uses his actual name, Ralph, to most acquaintances. He says, *"I am forever indebted to the Lord and the patience and love of His people."*

I, too, rejoice to witness what the Lord has done for this man. Today he is an ordained minister and a licensed school psychologist, with a lovely family. His criminal record was expunged.

Chapter Ten

I'm Free

"I was so weary, sick and tired of sin
It seemed to me my life was about to end.
I'd been running for so long
Just a fugitive,
But I knew there must be a better way to live"

© Sheldon Gooch, Patmos Records

In 1937, Bukka White, one of the great blues singers of
the American South, was recorded at Parchman Prison Farm
for the Library of Congress. He was serving three years for

shooting an assailant in the thigh. In 1947 and 1948, musicologist Alan Lomax walked alongside chanting prison chain gangs, recording them as they broke rocks in the hot sun on the Parchman Farm. Prisoner Henry Ratcliffe made history with his "field holler", and John Dudley gave us "Po Boy Blues" on his recording, titled *Negro Prison Songs*.

They were not the first famous blues singers to serve time in Parchman; "Son" House did time for murder in 1928-29. The father of America's darling, Elvis Presley, was even incarcerated there in the same year as the Lomax recordings. The Mississippi Delta lies unchallenged as the birthplace of Blues music, with a multitude of now-famous singers once living within a few miles of Parchman: Muddy Waters, Charley Patton, B.B. King, Robert Johnson, John Lee Hooker – the list goes on and on. It is no coincidence that blues music is also filled with songs about life in prison, with songs like, "Chain Gang Blues," "County Jail," "Parchman Farm Blues," "Another Man Done Gone," and "Jailhouse Blues." Alan Lomax describes the music that is born in prison cells and work farms in this way:

These songs belong to the musical tradition which Africans brought to the New World, but they are also as American as the Mississippi River. They were born out of the very rock and earth of this country, as black hands broke the soil, moved, reformed it, and rivers of stinging sweat poured upon the land under the blazing heat of Southern skies, and are mounted upon the passion that this struggle with nature brought forth.

They tell us the story of the slave gang, the sharecropper system, the lawless work camp, the chain gang, the pen. "

In 1987, another convict of the Mississippi State prison system made a professional recording for Patmos Records, singing a song of freedom like no other. Clad in prison stripes and shuttled to the recording studio in an armored van, Sheldon Gooch joined with California producer Roby Duke to record *"I'm Free,"* a compilation of 10 songs that take blues music a notch above the ordinary by offering one thing that most prison songs don't: hope. Sheldon was my convict helper for many years, traveling all over the state with our speaking team, *Captives for Christ*. Rather than expressing merely the emotion and tragedy of a life gone wrong, Sheldon's message was one of freedom through Christ, though still bound by a life-plus-60-year sentence in earthly bondage.

When I first came on staff full-time at Parchman's Unit 29, Sheldon was one of the prisoner gym workers at "Castle Grayskull." My office being directly above the gymnasium, he could hardly avoid me, though he tried his utmost to do so. He later told me how much it irritated him when I would wave to him, speaking of God's love.

An accomplished athlete and black belt in karate, this handsome, intelligent black man from the ghettos of Detroit came to Mississippi to seek a better life, opening his own school of self defense. Bad habits from his youth soon led to a string of bad choices, including burglary, heroin use and the crime for which he was ultimately sent to Parchman: armed robbery.

Sheldon was feared by most of the other inmates and was suspected by security of drug selling and other illegal activities in the prison. No proof was ever forthcoming, though, and I found him to be charming and helpful when he finally let down his guard and allowed me to know him.

Because of his communication skills and bright personality, I invited Sheldon on many occasions to help with visiting ministers and teams of volunteers. He was constantly confronted with spiritual influence, though I did not discover until later that it was not foreign to him. He had grown up in the church, with the example of a godly mother, who was no doubt still praying for him.

On one occasion, an ex-hippie, rock-n-roll musician-turned-preacher named Joe Shelton came to a special service at Castle Grayskull. He told the story of Jesus in a style unlike any of the prisoners had ever expected before, and Sheldon actually *heard* the good news that Jesus loved him and died for him. Joe shared his own story and sang songs that he had written, including *"Tonight is the Night."* Touched by the Spirit of God, this tough convict who had little hope of ever getting out of prison began to shed tears in front of 500 other inmates who would ordinarily consider such emotion a sign of weakness.

Sheldon gave his life to Christ and experienced the forgiveness and love he desperately needed. Did he change? So dramatically and immediately that both convicts and staff were shocked and suspicious. Did he think it would get him out of prison? Time alone would tell.

Meanwhile, God was working on the other half of our future team of Captives for Christ. Joe Elliott had previously served a term in the famously tough Cook County Jail in Chicago. He had come to Mississippi, as he explained it, "to slow down." An expert pickpocket, he discovered that the crowds in our state were insufficient for him to continue in his chosen career path – so he turned instead to armed robbery. He was apprehended after robbing a drug dealer, who he assumed would not turn him in because of his own illegal activity. The man not only turned him in, but was delighted when Joe received an 80-year sentence.

The shock of such a long incarceration period brought him desolation and fear, causing him to call out to the God whom his Christian mother had tried to teach him about. He became a dedicated servant of Christ and eventually could even joke about his unusually long sentence, "*I heard that Mississippi was called the Hospitality State and I am convinced that it is true – because they have been extending it to me for years now!*" What a blessing Joe became in my life, and remains to this day. He writes his tesimony in Chapter 13 of this book.

Our Deputy Warden at Unit 29 was Raymond Roberts, who proved to be a dedicated, extremely competent leader. He expected his staff to be equally devoted and did not fail to recognize those who were diligent and effective. I loved having a boss who was visible and available, even when he was absorbed in the enormous task of running our "prison within a prison." He appreciated the Chaplain's Department and encouraged me to provide a strong, spiritual program.

It was, therefore, with much disappointment that I received the news that Raymond would be leaving Parchman to become Superintendent of the brand new prison being built near the capitol city of Jackson. The new prison would house the entire population of female prisoners in the state, as well as be the Reception Center for all convicts entering the penal system. The new convicts would be kept in Maximum Security cells until they were classified, and then moved to permanent housing at Parchman or one of the other satellite programs scattered around the state.

I knew that Unit 29 would greatly feel the absence of Raymond's leadership, and cringed at the possible replacements, any of whom could easily be hostile to a spiritual environment. It never occurred to me to apply for the position of Chaplain at the new prison, until Raymond suggested it. I knew that the competition would be fierce, as indeed it was. I asked that the Lord's will be done, not wanting to push myself into any position outside of His divine plan. Much to my surprise, I was selected to accompany Raymond and his staff as head of the new Chaplain's department.

With the organizational skills I had developed from beginning the program at Unit 29, I certainly had the experience to tackle the job, but the unknown is nonetheless somewhat unsettling, and the new prison was in an area that I had never even visited. Leaving the only town I had lived in permanently since coming to America, I packed my belongings and said goodbye to the loyal friends who had shared in my tragedies and triumphs over the decades.

When I walked onto the grounds of what was originally called the Rankin County Correctional Facility, it was far from completed, but the staff had plenty to do. They met daily in the finished firehouse to write policies and procedures, interview staff, and prepare for the convicts who would arrive as soon as the buildings received their final touches. I also visited local church ministries to acquaint them with the needs of the new prison.

There were no positions yet allocated for assistant chaplains, or even for a secretary in our department. I knew that I could not keep up with everything alone. With the first 140 male inmates soon be selected, I hesitantly asked if Sheldon Gooch and Joe Elliott could be transferred to become my helpers. *"I will let them come, Wendy,"* agreed Raymond, *"but I don't trust those gangsters, and I will watch them closely."*

Chapter Eleven

Wendy's Gangsters

*"Look, the men you put in jail
are standing in the temple courts,
teaching the people."*

Acts 5:25 KJV

By the time I retired in 1998, there were more than 2000 males, 1000 females and a large staff of employees at the new prison. It had been renamed as the Central Mississippi Correctional Facility (CMCF), and it remains today the thriving counterpart to the original Parchman farm. It was not until the number of inmates reached into the thousands that I was given a secretary and, after many requests, another chaplain. I was on call 24/7 and remained at the prison for 12 to 14 hours each day. Raymond had kept his word, though, and allowed "my gangsters" from Parchman, Sheldon and Joe, to be transferred as my helpers at the Chaplain's Department.

Looking around the new prison one day, I noted all the brand new buildings that had been deemed desirable and necessary for a functioning penal institution. One thing was sadly missing, though: there was no chapel. In this place of punishment and pain, there was no structural symbol of forgiveness and hope. The state does not allocate funds for spiritual facilities, but that did not stop me from determining that there *would* be a chapel. I doubt that any Warden other than Raymond Roberts would have been as open-minded, but he gave his support and enthusiasm to my ever-evolving fundraising efforts to build a chapel on the prison grounds. Permission was granted from all the proper authorities, and the "Chapel Fund" was established.

The convicts were thrilled about the possibility of having a real chapel, rather than meeting in the stark dining halls with immovable metal benches. They were eager to help in any way, and I now recognize this enthusiasm as the beginning seeds of the powerful outreach ministries that were to be formed from within the circles of convict believers. They poured their energies into contributing, in large ways or small, to a common goal. Perhaps for the first time, these inmates began to feel the satisfaction that comes from working together, and believing in the power of God to remove obstacles.

They worked hard. Dozens of women sewed handcrafted items, and the men used their skills in leatherwork and carpentry to make saleable items for the chapel fund. We held rummage sales in the parking lot at the prison, with items donated by churches and individuals, and sold hot dogs and hamburgers to the prison employees.

While the prisoners were doing their part on a daily basis, many private citizens heeded the call, hundreds of them sending monthly contributions. After newspaper and television publicity, some individuals, such as Linda Drivas from Jackson, gave large amounts to speed up the accumulation of our funds. Stuart Irby, Jr., the well-known philanthropist who contributed in many other ways to our ministry as well, was exceedingly generous is his support for our venture.

It was during this time period that Sheldon recorded his gospel album, with some of our country's best musicians providing the music on tracks recorded in California, and then flown to the studio in Jackson. The proceeds from the sale of this recording entered the Chapel Fund. The title song from the album, *I'm Free,* was also the theme song for the radio program we developed. From that program, we received many invitations to visit churches with our speaking team, to share our need for a chapel.

For about two years, we were on the air regularly, with Sheldon handling the taping of the show, and me interviewing Christian convicts. It was unrehearsed and quite a new venture for me. It took several weeks before I realized that I could just be myself, stumbling or saying the wrong things occasionally, and that it was okay to laugh at our mistakes.

I still remember one broadcast when one of our young females made the statement that she was a thief, but acknowledging, *"I know now that this was a character deficiency."* I suppose that some self-help group must have taught her to tie up her crime in such a tidy little coined phrase. *"Honey, the Bible calls that stealing,"* I explained on the air, *"and it is a sin, not a character deficiency."* We received lots of mail from that particular program – and *most* listeners agreed with me.

One day I approached Raymond in his office and said enthusiastically, *"I have an idea!"* He bowed his head and groaned, *"Oh no, not another one."*

"I want to do a TV show titled, "As the Chaplain Turns," I responded. He just stared at me for a moment, before we both broke out in laughter. This one was a joke – though the months before we broke ground for our chapel did hold many more adventures in fundraising. Raymond always listened, and for the most part, gave his approval.

Finally, the day came to begin construction. With about one-third of the needed funds already raised, I took a leap of faith and broke ground, trusting that God would provide the remaining funds. The convicts with Trustee status were allowed to volunteer their help, and many did, even after working their normal prison jobs all day. I was as proud as any "mother" could be, watching my "gangsters" climb all over that Chapel, toiling in the burning sunshine of the Mississippi skies. The air was filled with the sound of their labors, as well as their joy, with laughing and joking, and often the hearty sounds of hymns being sung to the heavens. Free-world volunteers mingled with the inmates, many of them donating their time as well as their money. It was a glorious, spiritual time, one that no doubt affected the atmosphere of the prison for many years to come. Though the Department of Corrections may have quickly forgotten how that chapel came into being, and the sacrifices of the convicts in making it a reality, I will always remember. And God will reward them.

That first chapel was really quite utilitarian, but we embraced it deeply. It immediately filled its purpose of providing a sanctuary for worship, meeting places and a real home for the chaplain's offices. After a few years, we raised funds once again to build a large sanctuary. The day that the steeple arrived for the finished building is a picture that is still bright in my mind. The day was beautiful, with brilliant blue skies and puffy white clouds overhead. When the steeple was hoisted onto the roof, a convict named Johnny attached it into its proper place. He then raised his hands in victory, as this symbol of freedom pointed toward heaven.

I had not had the privilege of choosing the chapel's location, and it was not really to my liking – but as the prison grew and more housing units were added, I found, to my great delight, that our chapel was right smack in the middle of everything. God's plan is always perfect.

I have been asked more than once how I knew that God wanted me to build a chapel. The normal duties of a prison chaplain are so all-consuming that I simply could not have added fundraising and planning a construction project, if it had not been for the supernatural stamina the Lord gave me during that time period. There were many nights when I fell exhausted into bed, thanking Him for giving me the strength to continue.

I wish I could say that I had heard a voice from the heavens saying, *"Build!"* or even that I had received an obvious "sign" from God that I was to take on such a huge task. All I can say is that I saw a need and jumped in to meet it. In all my years of serving our Lord, I can say that this has almost always been the way that He has spoken to me. I did try to discern my own motives, making sure to do what brings honor to Him, which is not always easily ascertained.

Life seems to be on hold in a prison, with only the past and the future of any value. But, Christian convicts do not need to feel that service to their Lord and fellow man can only begin *"when I get out."* During the construction of our chapel, I saw an answer to my prayer of many years that the men and women in my care could somehow use their time in useful, challenging ways.

There was great excitement in the air now as, over the next few months, God brought forth what came to be known as *Inside Ministries.* Incarcerated Christians began to recognize their God-given talents, and were given an opportunity to use them. They began to realize their own worth and the contribution that they could make to society through their Lord. From the inside out, God's spirit began to move across our state, as the least likely of all God's children shared His love. Programs within the prison, as well as outside their gates, were established. My two convict helpers, Joe and Sheldon, spent countless hours organizing this new ministry. I was the sponsor or overseer, but to the extent that they were allowed, they did most all of the planning.

A perfect prison record, a Christian testimony, and an ability to sing were required for one of our first outreach ministries, an all-male traveling choir. They called themselves "Song of a Soul Set Free." I remember gathering in the parking lot with these men, on our first outing into the community, to sing at a local church. They were all well-groomed and wearing special t-shirts, their prison uniforms neatly pressed. We bowed our heads in prayer and when they looked up, I said, *"Okay, if anyone is thinking of escaping, you must tell me first, so that I can go with you. Because I am NOT returning without each and every one of you!"* The guards accompanying us were taken aback by that statement, but the guys just laughed. *"Aw, Chaplain, we ain't goin nowhere,"* one of them said.

My own musical abilities are confined to a great appreciation for the gifts of *others,* and so I recruited the gracious help of Phil and Marty Odom, then later Bert and Suzanne Stanton of the Crossgates Baptist Church in Brandon, to lead its choir. The members of "Song of a Soul Set Free" performed in churches and in the prison, gaining recognition for their talent and glorifying God in harmonious praise.

Since most convicts do not have the custody status that allows departure from the grounds of the prison, many used their talents inside the walls. Those with a talent for writing began a newsletter. In addition to encouraging their own creative abilities, they were able to lift the spirits of fellow convicts with short testimonies, poetry and humorous stories from the convict population. We also used the newsletter to inform readers, both on the inside and out, of all religious activities provided by the Chaplains Department. The printing of the publication was done at Mississippi College, funded by the *Beginning Again in Christ* prison ministry.

Another group of convicts planned and led devotionals for a church service on visiting days. For about 30 to 40 minutes, families could bring incarcerated loved ones to worship. The children gathered there were delighted with skits written by the convicts, and performed with much gusto. Volunteers came in and trained our convicts in the art of puppetry, which they used to entertain young and old alike. The prison maintenance department constructed a puppet theater, and some of our puppets were even dressed in prison uniforms.

Ann, a very gifted female inmate, wrote and directed plays with meaningful, effective messages. The convicts were especially thrilled to perform for the prison staff, including the wardens. They were allowed to wear costumes over their prison garb, but it was not unusual to see the bottom layers of prison uniforms peeping out from beneath a Jesus robe.

An inside speaking team, comprised of Medium Custody convicts, talked to touring youth groups. County Judge James Smith (who later became a state Supreme Court Judge) sent several groups of youthful offenders to the prison to "open their eyes." He wrote to the Superintendent (the new title for Warden) that our program was much appreciated by the Court, proclaiming, *"I believe the evidence has already indicated that the program is highly successful and is producing the desired results."*

The convicts involved with Inside Ministries also sponsored a World Vision child, and very diligently collected the monthly financial donations. They continued this support until the state no longer allowed convicts to have money in their possession.

Each convict involved in Inside Ministries gave of themselves sacrificially, and I saw them mature in their faith, as they were given a chance to contribute. They learned to rejoice in their differences, and understand the importance of each member of society. They learned that everyone has a function as part of the Body of Christ, as described in I Corinthians, Chapter 12.

For all those ministering quietly (or otherwise!) inside the walls of captivity, there were equal works of God being performed on the "outside." Though they lived and worked at the prison, there was a group of inmates approved for travel with the Chaplains Department, and they comprised the foundation of our "Captives for Christ" speaking team. With lives that were once so broken and useless, these men and women brought insight from their own experiences to many "free" people who were in despair. Their message was centered around the concept that Jesus was the only true and effective deliverance from the many forms of imprisonment.

After careful and prayerful consideration, I would choose the convicts to be included on the team. In addition to the state's requirements, my own criteria for consideration included a consistent and exemplary commitment to Christ while in prison. The recommendations went to the Classification Committee for examination, and to the Superintendent for a final decision.

A licensed counselor, Richard Pride, volunteered his time to conduct workshops for our team members. He taught them skills for recognizing and interacting with various types of individual behavior. One desire of the team was to encourage young people to open up during the one-on-one aspect of the program. My contributions in their training included suggestions in public speaking, and appropriate ways to share their story. Depending on the audience, the comfort level of people in the room with convicts can vary widely. *"Don't tell little old ladies the gory details,"* I suggested, and *"don't preach – simply tell what God has done in your life."* I emphasized that they were also not to give the devil or their past any glory by dwelling too much on the years of their criminal activities.

There was never a need to remind the *Captives for Christ* team to conduct themselves in an exemplary manner. They were very aware that they were representing not only the prison and the Chaplains Department, but also their Lord. There were occasional embarrassing moments when an individual talked too long, dragging the service or assembly out past their designated quitting time. Yet, in the 20 years that I took this team all over the state of Mississippi, there was never one negative incident. There was, occasionally, some opposition from those who did not understand. Some politicians once raised the issue of "public safety," questioning the wisdom of allowing "people of their nature" to go out into the community at large. After a presentation to a Legislative delegation, and a review by the Corrections Commissioner, the decision was made that we should continue. The Commissioner judged that *the Captives for Christ program contributes significantly to convict rehabilitation*" and is "*well planned and presented.*"

I still have in my files hundreds of letters from civic clubs, churches, youth groups, schools, universities and even nursing homes, all thanking the team for the insights and impact of their visits. Some groups made our team a regular part of their activities, with the Open Door Church in Vicksburg inviting our team to join them every fifth Sunday. I will always be grateful to pastors George Hammett and Joe Shelton, and all the people there, for the warmth and genuine love to our guys and girls. In return for the prisoners' constant willingness to share their life story in the community, these people nurtured them with acceptance and "the best food in the world."

Though we were always exhausted, especially on late night trips, the speaking engagements were, with rare exceptions, a source of great satisfaction and enjoyment. I always cautioned the teams not to appear *too* happy when returning to the prison, to prevent jealousy from those who were not included.

Unfortunately, there is still legalism, or strict adherence to the letter of the law, in some Christian circles. There were actually churches that would not welcome us because the females' uniforms included pants. On one such occasion, I managed to get special permission for the girls to wear plain, unattractive, long skirts for a Sunday morning service. We also, myself included, took off our make-up and earrings, teasing one another about the difference "a little paint" made! Our presentation touched so many lives that morning, and we were received with love. The reaction to the same stories, however, would have been negative had we not adapted to their standards of appearance. I still feel anger when recalling another time when just such a thing happened.

We were once invited to speak to a youth group in a rural area of Mississippi. Since it was a night service and it was for youth, I chose to wear jeans. My girls were often uncomfortable amongst people with the luxury of dressing well, and I decided to use this opportunity to make them feel less conspicuous than usual.

Our first clue that all was not well came when a deacon greeted our black team members with, *"You boys won't need that juke box in here."* It was a racial slur, calling them "boys," indicating feelings of superiority, in tones that were universally recognized as racist. There was no trace of warmth or welcome extended to us, and it was all very awkward. After sharing our testimonies, the pastor took over and proceeded to publicly humiliate my "babes" in Christ. He criticized our dress, totally ignoring the message of God's grace in the lives of these men and women.

I was furious. We could have walked away and learned a lesson in forgiveness, or humility, or any number of acquired graces. But, these young Christians in my care could learn those things later – right now, I was going to stand up for them. The world is hard and punishing on its own, without the help of self-righteous hypocrites like these. I stood before his congregation and spoke from the Scriptures about our human righteousness being as filthy rags in God's eyes, and likened their harsh, critical words to the "clanging cymbals and noisy gongs" of I Corinthians, Chapter 13.

If I speak with the tongues of men and of angels, but do not have love, I have become a noisy gong or a clanging cymbal. And if I have the gift of prophesy, and know all mysteries and all knowledge; and if I have all faith, so as to remove mountains, but have not love, I am nothing.

This was not the only time we ever experienced racism, though most of the time it was merely inferred. The South was still licking its wounds from losing countless battles during the Civil Rights Movement of the 60s and 70s, and most people had either been enlightened or were wise enough to keep their mouths shut. We got more than our share of glances and glares, however. On speaking engagements where food was not provided, and driving times were long, we were allowed to go into restaurants for meals. I was sometimes the only white woman in the midst of black convicts, with a guard who was sometimes black as well. And to top it all off, most of them called me "Ma" when away from the prison! Sheldon was a fantastic actor, and could perfectly mimic the white redneck racist (only in private, of course). *"Lookie thar at that whaaat woman with them niggers,"* he would joke.

Joe was equally gifted in performance, and we never knew what antics he would perform, especially at youth meetings. He was known all over the prison and now all over the state, for his comedic abilities. Once, as a group of rather nervous trainee officers toured his building at the prison, he put his hands on the shoulders of another convict and stared ahead unblinking, pretending that he could not see. The trainees, particularly the females, were very concerned that a blind man was locked up and left to fend for himself in a crowded prison populace. I don't know how amused they were or weren't upon discovering that his eyesight was perfect.

Some of our moments together out in "the world" were poignant, others intense, and some just plain sad. Humor was equally as prevalent, though, and it is those moments I remember with great fondness. One hilarious incident took place in a fairly staid church, when two inmates were singing together. It was a very touching moment, filled with emotion – until the girl's new false teeth fell out. She handled it extremely well, scooping up the falling teeth and putting them in her pocket, as she continued to sing. It was all we could do to keep a straight face through the rest of the service.

On our way out to another speaking engagement one day, we had barely gotten down the road when one of the guys said, *"Ma, I have to go to the bathroom."* In my best motherly voice, I scolded him, asking, *"Why didn't you go before you left home?"* Without missing a beat, he replied, *"I did – but that was three years ago."* This was a guy with a very long sentence for robbing a bank with only a note saying, *"Hand over the money."* Unknown to the employees of the bank, he was more afraid than they were.

There were also more than a few tears as these men and women shared the stories of their lives. Many had grown up in poverty and neglect, and some of the women had stories of sexual molestation that chilled my relatively protected soul. Many became prostitutes at an early age to acquire money for drug addictions. One lived on the streets from the age of 13, after escaping from an abusive home situation. Pauline "scammed" money for a cult leader, who enticed her with promises of prosperity. Jean, in prison for killing her husband, would always cry when recounting the abuse she received from his hand, and the remorse she felt for exacting her own revenge. It was so hard for me to understand why she didn't just leave. I learned, however, that in almost every case of abuse, it was various levels of fear that kept them from leaving or going to the authorities.

Some got what they deserved, and others got more. There were unfair sentences at times, like Georgia receiving 60 years for a first offense of selling drugs. It was near a school zone. She was visibly crushed when a new convict arrived one day with the exact same conviction, but was given only 80 days in the military program. Though it is hard to accept injustice without bitterness, Georgia herself even said on occasion, *"God knew what He was doing."* She admitted to needing the shock of a long prison sentence to bring about her repentance. She served 15 years before being paroled.

The team members were from a variety of backgrounds, many poor and lacking in education. There were also those who came from prominent families, and some with college degrees. One young lady, the daughter of a judge, tearfully told how she had disappointed her family by repeated involvement in the drug culture. Sammie, articulate and educated and precise, had not been satisfied with a good living, but wanted riches. His life sentence, for a drug deal that ended in homicide, taught him that happiness is not in the amount of material possessions one can accumulate. Anne, an extremely gifted school teacher serving a 10-year sentence for armed robbery, told of her rebellion from a sexually abusive father who was both a college professor and a preacher. She had hidden the abuse in an attempt to protect her family.

The speaking team went through many changes over the years. We began by riding in private cars, then adapted to using secure state vehicles. From me alone as an escort, with a male volunteer when the convicts include males, and later with a security guard. The guards enjoyed this assignment, since the convicts were trustworthy and our hosts often provided good food. Our joy was contagious, with several officers experiencing spiritual changes in their own lives through their involvement with the Captives for Christ team.

Suddenly it was announced that only off-duty security officers could escort us, and we were greatly concerned that our ministry would be restricted. We could not afford to pay them. Instead, many were willing to accompany us without compensation. How thankful I was to them, and continue to be in memory. One officer, so willing to give of his time, was the world's worst driver. *"Ma, would you please drive?"* my tough convicts would plead. We were reminded of the Biblical story of lookouts seeing a cloud of chariot dust on the horizon and remarking, *"It must be Jehu, for he doth drive furiously."* I couldn't bring myself to hurt the officer's feelings, so I would whisper, *"Buckle up, and pray."* We always began each trip with prayer – but our prayers were most fervent when he was behind the wheel.

There are no longer any traveling teams from Mississippi prisons, and I am sorry to know that policies have changed so much since those days. I do realize, however, that there is a time for everything, and I am very thankful for being a part of such an exciting and beneficial era in the history of the Mississippi Department of Corrections.

Every team member in Captives for Christ regretted their crimes, and knew that they deserved the punishment they received. All agreed that coming to the end of themselves in prison was the best thing that could have happened to them. Although most Christians have not had to experience such severe consequences of crime, we all have to come to Christ in humility, admitting that our own goodness is not good enough.

At the close of each trip, after I had seen God use these men and women to minister His love to hundreds of "free" people, I would watch in sadness as they walked through the gates and razor-wired fences to re-enter the chaos of the prison buildings – while I drove away to the quiet haven of my home.

Chapter Twelve

Day In Day Out

Raymond Roberts, our prison Superintendent, was moving to Kansas. To use a very Southern expression, the entire staff went into a *Blue Funk*. Though we knew it was a good move for him, and understood why another state would entice this very capable man, we were crushed to lose his strong leadership. I think that our own state leaders failed to recognize what they had in this young man. Raymond retired as head of the Kansas prison system.

After Raymond, there were a series of wardens, each with their own personalities and leadership styles. The Chaplain's Department was sometimes appreciated, sometimes merely tolerated, and occasionally ignored. There were changes with each incoming leader, seemingly without thought to the consequences.

I always believed that God had sent me into the prisons to be His ambassador and that my concerns were spiritual, so I avoided getting embroiled in prison politics. My regular visits to the housing quarters of the convicts gave them an opportunity to talk, though, and so I would be constantly besieged with requests for help with family problems, complaints of unfair treatment, and mediation between convicts who were quarreling, etc.

I tried to keep my counseling in line with Biblical principles, referring matters outside my area of responsibility to other staff members. It is a common convict practice to play one employee against another, but I would not allow it. There were occasions, though, when obviously unfair treatment had to be addressed, and I would be pulled into the middle of a conflict. It is impossible to be loved by everyone, and so I'm sure I made occasional enemies, divided equally between inmates and staff.

While the *Inside Ministries* and *Captives for Christ* continued to flourish, the day-in, day-out chores of a prison chaplain continued. The prison grew into such a large institution that someone donated a golf cart for chaplains to ride around the prison grounds. One of the convicts carved wings out of wood and painted them gold, placing them on each side of the cart. Another made a sign that was posted on the front: *Soul Patrol*. I thoroughly enjoyed zooming around the prison in the Soul Patrol, acknowledging the enthusiastic response of the convicts to my "Queen Elizabeth" wave. The men also built a special pulpit for me, designed for my small stature, and I have used it even now in my retirement years.

One of the buildings I visited was for older and disabled females, many in their seventies and beyond. One lady there entered prison when she was in her eighties, for killing her boyfriend. She loved jewelry and adorned herself daily with several necklaces, rings and earrings, as well as a bow in her hair. Another older female won a battle with a younger convict in the cafeteria one day by biting off her finger. When I visited her in Maximum Security, I had to chastise her and speak of the unacceptability of her behavior. "*Ms. Chaplain,*" she said to me by way of explanation, "*that girl's finger just sort of got in my mouth.*" After trying to suppress a burst of laughter, I attempted to convince her that vengeance belongs to God and that He would repay. I'm afraid that she did not take me very seriously, as she muttered, "*Well, I bet she won't bother me again.*"

One of the wardens during this time period was particularly sympathetic and flexible if the needs were extreme. One of my male assistants was diagnosed with lung cancer. As he became increasingly ill, he begged me to help him stay there at CMCF, rather than being transferred to die in the hospital at Parchman. The warden somehow managed to honor my request on James' behalf. Not only was he allowed to stay, but an exception was made for me to bring special food to him, and to assist in making his final days more comfortable.

James did not come to know Christ in his heart until the last months of life. Though I talked with him on many occasions, he could not get past the idea that his lifestyle was too wicked for God to forgive. One day, he finally understood that Jesus came to earth because of our wickedness, and to compensate for our own inability to cancel our sin with His goodness. James gave his life to the One who died for him and loved him unconditionally. What a change in his life! One day I pushed him in his wheelchair to speak to a group of visiting teenagers. With tears streaming down his thin, sick face, he told them, *"Don't wait as long as I did."*

Early one morning while still at home, I received a call from the prison to come quickly. James was dying and asking for me. I was overcome with grief when I arrived too late, but was so happy to learn that he died with fellow Christians holding his hands and surrounding him with prayer. I spoke at his funeral, assuring his family that he was now free and with Jesus.

I will always have admiration in my heart for the Christian warden who allowed James to be with those who cared about him in those final days – and that he did not die alone. This same warden, Lake Lindsey, granted me permission to bring soup to a female convict in Maximum Security who was dying with AIDS. Only rarely does one find such compassion in a prison.

How often I have found myself saying, in response to questions about convicts, *"There but for the Grace of God go I."* They are simply people who have ruined their own lives by hurting others. And they pay the consequences for their crime and sin. During my tenure as a Chaplain for the Department of Corrections, rehabilitation was the buzzword. Sheldon was able to see what all their cultivated wisdom apparently could not: *"Rehabilitation means to restore to one's prior condition. But, I don't need to be what I previously was!"* Regeneration...making new...is the only chance for lasting change. Both in a prison, and in the world-at-large, only in Christ can regeneration occur. The Spirit of God enabled hundreds of convicts to become born again, cleansed by the blood of Christ, and given the chance to begin life anew.

Chapter Thirteen

God's Mercy

Prisons are hell on earth in so many ways, but there is a great difference. Prisons are not God-forsaken. Neither razor wire nor concrete, sophisticated locks, surveillance systems or cruel human beings, can keep God from penetrating hearts. The Spirit of God invades the noise and confusion of hundreds of housing units…or quietly enters the solitary cell. Those who call out to Him from their desperation are surrounded by His tender love.

We have all seen movies or read books and articles about the depravity in our nations' prisons – and they are, for the most part, accurate. However, in prison society as in the "free-world," the battle between good and evil rages. I have often told convicts, *"There are really only two races, believer and unbeliever."* It is always possible to change one's allegiance and I have seen, on numerous occasions, the impact the Gospel of Jesus Christ has in penal institutions. I have seen convicts gathered together in prayer, studying to obey his commandments; learning to love one another; doing good to those who spitefully use them; seeking to make restitution to those they have harmed; bringing peace into chaos. How privileged I have been to be a part of His people in prison.

Recently, while I was speaking to a group of people, describing the horrors of prison life, a lady angrily said, *"Well, that is just what they deserve."* My reply affirmed that I believe in punishment, but I reminded her that we are all guilty before God and many of us could easily be in the same situation. *"We should thank Him that our sin didn't land us in prison. We should daily bow before the One who made it possible for us to receive forgiveness; who makes it possible for us to avoid the punishment we all so richly deserve."*

In one of his inimitable songs, my friend Joe Shelton describes our attitude toward sinners: *"If I'd a been God, old Abe would be dead...old David would be dead...old Joe would be dead...but God's mercy endures forever."* I thank Him for the mercy that reaches "the most defiled."

Chapter Fourteen

After Prison

It was my desire in retirement that God would use me more in the latter years than ever before. In the past 17 years, that has been true, though not at all in ways that I anticipated.

Not long after I retired, I moved to the tiny lakeside town of Glen Allan, surrounded by endless cotton fields that once thrived as vast plantations of the antebellum South, now joined by the relatively new crops of rice, soybeans, wheat and corn. Upon first arrival, I stayed with my friends T.C. and Ann Woods, who had purchased and restored Mount Holly, the elaborate rural Italianate architectural style mansion built by slave labor in the mid-1800's. During my years working in the prison, this was often my retreat from the constant activity and pressure of prison responsibilities. In this beautiful, peaceful abode on lovely Lake Washington, I always felt relaxed and refreshed. Ann remembers that I "always slept a lot there."

Construction on Mount Holly began before the Civil War, waning and rising, on and off, during the deadly conflict between countrymen of North and South, brother against brother. During General Sherman's fiery march through the South, burning hundreds of elaborate plantation homes to the ground, Mount Holly was spared, reportedly due to a personal relationship with Margaret Johnson Erwin, the female owner of the plantation. In her diary, discovered and published many years after her death, Margaret gives a personal account of William Tecumseh Sherman, as well as Henry Clay, visiting Mount Holly in the tumultuous years leading up to the declaration of Civil War.

In the 20th century, Mount Holly was once owned by the family of Shelby Foote, the Pulitzer Prize-winning Civil War historian, and it was placed on the National Register of Historic Places in 1970.

After being abandoned and neglected for decades, this 30-room mansion was acquired by my friend Ann. She and her husband T.C. lovingly restored Mount Holly to its former glory with period antiques and décor, preserving the curving staircases, wooden balustrades and original grand ballroom. The semi-hexagonal windows with carved lintels, 14-foot ceilings, 2-foot thick walls and ornate iron balcony of Mount Holly all stand in stark contrast to the plain flatness of the Mississippi Delta farmlands.

Entering through the Palladian type archway in the center pavilion always felt to me as though I was being transported back to a land and a time long forgotten, the grand and genteel South that existed for white plantation and slave owners long before I ever stepped foot into the Delta. The land surrounding Glen Allan is still owned and farmed by descendants of these former landowners, though many acres were sold off to newcomers such as Ann.

History ran deep in this region and spilled over to new generations of sharecroppers in the 1900s, whose shabby cabins with no running water or bathrooms still dotted the cotton fields. In 1914, a baby boy was born to one of the sharecropping families in Rolling Fork, just 5 miles from my new home in Glen Allan. This baby would grow to become Muddy Waters, now hailed as one of the nation's most notorious blues singers and ranked Number 17 in *Rolling Stone* magazine's list of the 100 Greatest Artists of All Time. In August 1941, Alan Lomax recorded him for the same Library of Congress series of field recordings that featured the now-famous hollers and chants of prisoners on the chain gang at Parchman Prison Farm.

I came to Glen Allan after 30 years of serving God in Mississippi's prisons. From the frenetic energy and stark bleakness of captivity, where thousands of lives touched my own, I now found myself isolated in a much different way. Endless miles of cotton and corn; rocking chairs creaking lazily on back porches; and Sunday church picnics in a land of gentility were a shock to my system in many ways.

However, God was by no means finished with me. In 1998, after I was "paroled" from the Mississippi Department of Corrections, I moved to Glen Allan to help Ann with Strait Gate, a ministry she started as an outreach to troubled young women. It quickly overflowed to encompass disadvantaged children, primarily from the black community. I joined Ann to help run Strait Gate, along with Dr. Dick Thomae and his wife, Lil, retired missionaries; James and Carey Piggs, local African American business people; and Mary Cooper, a long-time member of the Glen Allan community. We worked tirelessly to make a difference, never actually knowing if our efforts were long-lasting or even temporarily fruitful.

We took an old school building and received donations of money and labor to make it useful again, using the facility to open a food bank, teach GED classes, conduct Bible studies, and occasionally offer free medical services.

I dusted off an old talent of mine from childhood and started teaching tap dancing classes to the young children, most of whom had never participated in formal lessons of any kind in their lives, much less dancing. A dance supply store near Memphis donated dozens of pairs of tap shoes to our kids, and the *tip-tap-tapping* of tiny feet echoed through the cotton fields on hot summer afternoons. Young voices rang out with tunes like *"You're a grand ole flag, you're a high-flying flag—and forever in peace may you wave—you're an emblem of, the land I love, the land of the free and the brave."*

It must have been an odd sight indeed for anyone passing by, a 70-year-old white woman with a very British accent, belting out allegiance tunes to the American flag, with a troop of tap dancing black children following like a colloquial version of the Pied Piper.

I stayed in Glen Allan for eight years before moving back to Cleveland, the town where I had lived my life for so many years after arriving in America – first as a country club socialite and prominent attorney's wife, then driving the country roads to Parchman Prison every day; all while raising my four children, then sending them off to college and lives of their own.

After being gone for more than 20 years now, there were many adjustments to be made and many spiritual lessons still to be learned.

The emphasis for a significant number of American Christians, and certainly for me, is on "doing" things for His kingdom. So what would I "do" now, with a lot of time, but with the limitation of physical disabilities? One day this question was answered for me in a way I did not anticipate, when I read a passage from "*My Utmost for His Highest*," a devotional book by Oswald Chambers. "*It's not about doing,*" it said, "*but about being.*"

Those seven words made me rethink my goals for the latter part of my life. They also caused me to re-examine the Scriptures, where I discovered that so much of what I believed could actually be chalked up to "tradition."

I don't doubt that God has been involved in every moment of my life, from my days on the fishing wharves in Leigh-On-Sea to the years of evacuation in the English countryside during WWII; from my marriage and motherhood, to laboring to bring God's healing power to the captives of sin and crime. But I now also believe that an emphasis on works (not *for* salvation, but *after* it) had also diminished my desire to become more like Christ – though Scripture clearly teaches that we are to be conformed to His image (Romans 8:28, for one example).

Now I see that becoming more like Jesus creates the flow of concern for the physical, social and eternal destiny of humanity. For several years now I have yearned and prayed, as Paul did in Philippians Chapter 3: *"I want to know God."*

Time Served has meant many things in my life. My first book, *"Doing Time: Devotions,"* was written for prisoners still paying for their crimes in our nation's correctional institutes. In this book, I have reflected on my own life and how I have done my own time, with varying amounts of significance and impact, for more than 80 years. Perhaps before I leave this earth, I will have yet more to say about *Doing Time* in my old age, learning the things that I should have known much earlier.

Chapter Fifteen

His Amazing Grace

I am now, in my eighties, able to look back over the years and see much of what God has done in one ordinary life. Do I believe He is in control? Absolutely! Do "all things work together for good to those who love God and are called according to His purpose?" (Romans 8:28). Yes, absolutely – if we understand what His good is: to make His people like Him! "To conform His people to His image." (Romans 8:29).

The numerous lessons I have learned in these latter years far surpass what the "busy" years taught me. I am sometimes shocked to realize that so much of what I accepted during the most active periods was baby food at best, with a mixture of tradition. Not necessarily false, but certainly lacking. I have had to decide whether to include some of these thoughts in this narrative or, perhaps, write a future "Doing Time – the Latter Years." I will pray for His direction.

I thank you who are reading what God has done in my life and I believe you will say, "He has done wonderful things in my life as well." Please share them. Christians love to know about the lives their God has touched, and others need to hear. I am merely one of multitudes to whom God Has made Himself known and granted the gift of new life.

Those who read this narrative because they know me, in one capacity of another, will attest to my imperfections, and I know that but for the Grace of God, there would be no story. The presently incarcerated and ex-offenders who know Him will smile and remember how He penetrated the prison walls of their hearts and brought peace into their chaotic lives.

I pray for those of you in prison who, whether out of curiosity or boredom, find yourself reading these pages, that the Spirit of the real, living Jesus, will draw you to Himself. What He has done for me and for my convict friends, He can do for you.

To my family, near and far, I ask your forgiveness for the times I have failed you. I do my best to be a faithful servant of Jesus and I ask for your prayers that He will continue to work in my life to make me worthy of His name.

I urge all who do not know Him to pray for His forgiveness and surrender their lives to Him to bring Him honor and to receive what He is so ready to give – an assurance of an abundant life with Him after death.

Testimonies

"Blessed is he whose transgression is forgiven,
Whose sin is covered."

Psalms 32:1 KJV

Everyone who is paroled vows they will never return to prison. Recidivism is high, though, and rehabilitation programs are not always successful. Against advice, they go back to old friends and old habits, thinking that it won't happen to them again. The Apostle Paul said, in II Corinthians 5:17, that any man who is in Christ is a new creation. Most who come to know the Lord in prison do faithfully live for Him upon their release. Do I believe they all live sinless lives? Of course not. There are too many Biblical examples of God's people who fail – and my own history of imperfection. But, those who have loving concern from other believers and churches who support them, usually do make it.

Here, in their own words, are the stories of God's forgiveness and the testimonies of their new lives in Him. I was tempted to write these wonderful stories of redemption myself, but I believe that God will receive the greater glory as they speak in their own words, even though it may bring them pain to do so.

Sylvia

I come from what most people thought was a good family. We weren't rich. We weren't poor. We went to church. My sister and I were honor roll students. What no one knew was that there was abuse in the home – my Father physically, my Mother mentally and sexually.

As we grew older, I began to rebel. I hated both parents. They divorced when I was nine. We stayed with our Mother.

I got involved in the occult, using Ouija boards, séances and witchcraft books. I had Satanist acquaintances. I was out to prove to the world how mean, evil and cruel I was. In my experience, only those who were evil and cruel prevailed.

I remember when I started saying that I was going to kill my Mother. At first, I just wanted attention. I said many things for shock value alone. We had a physical confrontation. I had been told to go to my room while I was in the process of taking my prescribed medication. I finished taking it, and started to my room. My Mother decided to drag me there to make a point. Three times we scuffled. Three times I broke free, trying to get to my room. When I finally got there, the police were called. My Mother's story was different from mine. The police told me, *"Young lady, you are in Mississippi. Your Mother can do anything she wants to you as long as she doesn't leave any marks."* I knew then that no one was going to help me. My Mother was too clever to leave any marks – except the ones in my heart, my soul.

I went to school the next day, saying I would kill my Mother. An acquaintance of mine, whose approval I longed to have said, "W*hy don't you?"*

I think she didn't take me seriously and was hoping she would quiet my incessant complaints about my Mother. I said, *"I can't kill her, they would catch me."*

She said, *"If there is someone sick in your family, you could use their medication to do it."*

I thought, *"My Dad is on a breathing machine. All I'd have to do to kill him is turn the machine off."* Then I added, *"My sister is on insulin."*

"That's perfect," she told me.

I then started telling anyone who would listen that I had a plan to kill my Mother. My therapist listened to my plan. We ended up having a conference about it, the three of us: she, my Mother and me. I shrugged it off. I decided I'd leave when I was 18. I resorted to writing poetry about my hatred for my Mother and about her death.

Then, one night in the summer of 1992, my sister awakened me in need of emergency medical attention. My Mother didn't want to take her to the hospital. I ran to the phone to call my Grandmother for help. My Mother was right behind me and disconnected the phone. My sister was finally taken to the hospital after I was dropped her off at my Grandmother's apartment in the next town. When Melissa finally arrived at the hospital, a cyst on her spine was minutes from rupturing. When I visited her in the hospital she said, "*I feel I can't live with things the way they are. I can't live if Mom is alive. Will you kill her?*" I said I would.

It wasn't long before my sister and I figured out that we were not capable of killing her. Someone else would have to do it. I asked my boyfriend and he refused. I asked Melissa's current boyfriend. He said he would. On July 7, 1992, he did. We were all arrested that day on murder charges and later convicted. I was 17. Her boyfriend was 16, and my sister was 15.

Prison didn't change me very much. I planned my suicide from the first day. I continued promiscuous behavior with male convicts and officers. I became involved in homosexuality. I was miserable.

In February of 1995, I took 52 pills called Sinequan. When I woke up two days later, in the hospital on Valentines Day, I couldn't believe I wasn't dead. I was furious, and started planning again how I would kill myself. Suddenly, I felt this awesome presence fill the room. I felt a voice speak to my heart, "*No, you're not going to do this anymore. I love you. I have a plan for you, and there is a reason for you to be alive.*" I knew it was God, and I realized that He is the only reason I survived. Everything that all those Christians had told me about Him was true! I needed Jesus because I was a sinner. I needed to let Him be Lord of my life…the only one who had control of my life. I said "yes" to God that day.

Later, I began to say no to promiscuity, suicidal thoughts, homosexuality, occultism; the list goes on. The chaplain, whom I had once avoided, drew me into her Bible study group. I was blessed by her Godly wisdom and the teaching of many of the volunteers that she drew to the prison. I thank God for people like them – people who took the time to tell a rebellious, sinful young woman about a man named Jesus, who alone has the power to save and change.

A poem by Sylvia:

"Indigo"
A dark, bare, winter tree scrawls
Toward the indigo sky.
The lights wink at me like stars
A sunburst of moisture around each one.
I don't see the razor-wire when I look up.
All I see is Indigo.
I walk fast.
The voices of the crowd fade away.
I breathe deep – the sharp air biting my nose.
I am alone again with you, Lord.
It's just you and me.
Finally

After her conversion, Sylvia was a consistent witness for Christ, active in the spiritual life of the prison. She wrote poetry and shared her talent in art and interpretive dance with fellow prisoners. She was finally released after serving many years in prison, and lives a quiet life as a devoted believer in Christ. Sylvia's sister won an appeal for a new trial and was released after serving several years. She became an active member of Crossgates Baptist church in Brandon, Mississippi, where she was accepted and loved. She passed away recently after years of battling diabetes.

Sammie

Being born in the Bible belt of Mississippi, I was brought up in church all my life. As a child, and later a teenager, I did all the things that children do growing up, including sex and experimenting with drugs.

At age 19, I was the father of two children, married and in the Navy, trying to support my family. At this point, my experiences with life got serious. I developed a drug habit, a sex addiction (pornography), and a general wasting of my life.

After my discharge from the Navy I brought these new habits home with me, where I tried to appear normal. I went to school and started a career, and did all the things a model citizen did, including volunteer work and charity contribution. But like all lies, the one I was living was eventually revealed. One night, my gambling habit led to a situation that ended in someone's death. My life, which had been spiraling downward, hit bottom as I ended up in the

Mississippi State prison, with a 30-year sentence for manslaughter.

While in city jail, waiting to be transferred to the State prison, I heard a sermon like so many other I had heard over the years, only I really heard it this time, and it caused me to take a long look at my life and myself. It was during this time of reflection that I realized my need for Christ as my Savior, and I gave my life to Him. This was more than "jail house religion." I didn't care if I ever got out, as long as I didn't have to live as I had for so long.

For the first four years of my sentence, I was content to be saved and to share my salvation with anyone who would listen, and then I became a part of a prison ministry team called "Captives for Christ." This team's main purpose was to take the message of Christ to the community outside the prison walls and to show those who thought they were free that you don't have to be in a prison cell to be locked up. There are many personal prisons that have people from all walks of life bound up and far from free. That ministry helped all of its participants to grow through the sharing of our faith, because faith is like a muscle; the more you exercise it, the stronger it becomes.

Many who were a part of the "Captives" team got released miraculously and have stayed committed to Jesus, which is a testimony for Christ in itself. I am forever thankful to the One who gave me spiritual eyes to see and a new life in Him.

Sammie was gifted with a beautiful voice, which he used to the glory of God in churches. He was a respected member of society, with a responsible job in the medical field. He went to be with the Lord in 2012, after suffering a fatal heart attack.

Kenny

My name is Kennith "Pete" Williams. I grew up in a housing project in Birmingham, Alabama. There was a lot of hate in that place, but there was also a lot of good. We had our own little church where all the kids went to Sunday School. My mother and father did their best to instill good values in me, and for the first few years of my life, I was a quiet kid who stayed out of trouble.

By the time I was 12, however, I had begun drinking and taking drugs. It would be a long time before I finally realized the power that drugs and alcohol…and the devil, had over my words and actions during those years. At 17, I was doing heroin and really on my way to a life of hell.

A few months later, I was kicked out of school, and joined the Navy. My drug habit worsened, and I stayed in trouble. Although I managed to make it out of the Navy with an honorable discharge, the god of this world had blinded my mind (I Corinthians 4:4). After my discharge, I started stealing and robbing, doing anything I could to relieve the sickness and pain the drugs put on me.

Soon, I began robbing drug stores to support my habit. Finally, I was arrested in Alabama, Georgia and Mississippi, and was put into jail. I was almost relieved, thinking I would at least get some help with my drug problem. But I was wrong. I was charged with several drug store robberies and sentenced to a total of 105 years and was facing two life sentences without parole. In November of 1979, I went to prison for the first time in my life. If my life had been bad before, it was really a nightmare now.

That first year in prison, I tried to get off the drugs. For a while, I did okay. But the devil kept whispering, "You can do them just once or even every now and then. It'll be okay." Of course, that was a lie, and soon I was using drugs more than ever.

I was moved to a different unit within the prison. A few nights later, I saw some men gathering into a group. I figured there was going to be a fight. After a while, they all started to look over at me. Then one of them walked over and asked if I would like to come pray with them. I told him to get out of my face, or there really was going to be a fight! I told him I didn't need God, that I was going to die in this place. Of course, that was just what the devil wanted me to believe. Night after night, the same thing happened: One man would come over to my bed and tell me Jesus loved me. Then he would go and kneel down by his bed. I knew he was praying for me, and I wanted to kill him.

Then one night as I lay on my bed, a strange thing happened. God began to convict me of all the bad things I had done in my life. I realized the pain and suffering I'd been through wouldn't begin to compare with what was ahead of me if I didn't make some changes, and make them quickly. That night, in February of 1986, I asked the Lord to forgive me and to come into my life. And He did! He delivered me from drugs and helped me start all over again. *"If any one is in Christ, he is a new creation; the old has passed away, behold, the new has come."* (II Cor. 5:17 KJV).

I started studying God's Word and singing in our prison chapel services. I began sharing what the Lord had done for me with the other inmates and saw Him work in their lives too. While I was there in prison, I completed almost three years of Biblical studies.

Slowly the Lord restored my life, and in February of 1996 I was released, having served almost 17 years in prison. There have been some tough times. It isn't easy adjusting to the "free world" and starting all over again after you've been locked up for so many years. But God has always been right there beside me.

My first real job was with a painting company. By June of 1996, I owned the company. Seven months later, God called me into a prison ministry. Although ex-prisoners are not usually allowed to minister in the prisons of Mississippi unless they have been out for a number of years, I was given special permission to do a service once a month. Now I'm conducting five prison meetings each month in the Central Mississippi Correctional Facility and in prisons around the United States, plus speaking in churches and sharing my testimony in the drug awareness programs in schools. Wherever and whenever God opens the door, I'm there to tell others that they, too, can be delivered and set free by His love and grace and power.

The Bible says, *"Therefore if the Son makes you free, you shall be free indeed."* (John 8:36 KJV). I thank the Lord for taking away the drugs and setting me free. It is only now that I have Jesus that I have really begun to enjoy life. He told us this is the reason He came, that we *"might have life and have it more abundantly."* (John 10:10 KJV).

If you are bound by drugs or alcohol or lost in sin and think there is no way out, believe me, Jesus is the way! He said, *"I am the WAY, and the TRUTH and the LIFE."* (John 14:6 KJV). Whatever your problem, He is waiting to set you free!

Call on Him today, and pray this prayer, as I did there in my prison cell: "Lord Jesus, I am a sinner in need of a Savior. I'm truly sorry for my sins. I believe You are the Son of God, and that You died for me that I might have a new life in You. Please forgive me now, and help me start all over again." If you mean that with all your heart, you are born again, and Jesus is your Lord.

Kenny was eventually released from prison and became the director of "Captives Set Free Ministries." He was a faithful servant of Jesus and a dear friend of mine until he went to be with the Lord after a heart attack at a relatively young age.

Note: Kenny's testimony includes a continued fight to overcome drugs during his first year in prison. At the time, it was commonly acknowledged amongst prisoners that the source of these drugs infiltrating the penitentiary was the prison guards themselves.

Ann

At 55 years of age, I look back on my life and see how much has been wasted. The mental health profession would have a field day in my head, and even then I doubt I would know more than I have come to know through introspection and the illumination of the Holy Spirit. No, there's been no rent in the sky, no great thunderclap or revelation…God's voice has not yelled out to me. What has happened is that I have yielded to His desires for my life, and finally I accept as fact that you simply cannot live your life as your own.

The crux of my life-long problem, I now understand, is my human Father, who sexually abused me. The difference is that I no longer blame, and no longer use it as an excuse. I simply put it all down to part of the past.

There is no doubt that the abuse from my father had a powerful impact on my life. Now I see it clearly in many areas, including my refusal to ever lose weight, out of defiance of what he wanted me to look like (my four sisters were all trim and attractive.) I played drums; a very masculine choice – opposite the flute that fourteen friends played. I fought to go to Ole Miss (a "den of iniquity") and major in theatre and communications, not American history or English literature, as befits a lady! And let's not even talk about the men I chose.

Church? I am SO churched! As I grew up, I was surrounded by and immersed in church. I'm probably the only child to attend five vacation Bible schools each summer.

By age 3, I was teaching the character stories. Church was not an option; it was simply a ritual. Now, there's a nice word for you: ritual. Pretty much sums up religion to me, to this day.

My father was a minister and a professor at a Christian college. He was a thirty-three degree Mason. The community thought only the best of him. My mother was, in my opinion, a saint and the example of a true lady. I was so blessed to have her and the counterbalance that she brought to my life.

Because my four sisters and one brother were much older (grown) when I was born, I was raised much as a grandchild would be. The strict rules and conduct the older siblings grew up in were never applied to me, and it was only as an adult that I grasped why. My father wanted to keep me quiet, while my mother tried, in her own way, to keep the peace and somehow protect me. I understand now that incest was never thought about, much less discussed in the 1950's. What was done was to ship me off to New Orleans to live with my sister and to go to school. The reason given was that I was to be an "experiment" for Oschner Clinic for weight loss for children between ages 10 and 12, and I did lose 120 pounds. Trim and fit at age 13. Daddy's dream, I suppose!

I was out of the environment I had suffered in for the early years. However, by age 16 I returned, not just to home, but to the overweight teenager that still had to tolerate a father she loathed. I could never understand why my sisters ignored the situation – surely they knew? Or my mother – but I excused her from blame, because she was the one who I knew loved me, no matter what.

Church? I saw it as a pulpit for all my father stood for. If God allowed him to lead others, then there was something seriously wrong.

The advantage of living on a college campus as a young child was that I could "hang out" in any classroom and absorb what was being taught. Since the college was a mainline Christian college, the foundation in Bible history, theology, debate and the study of Biblical law was broad. However, the things I learned in those classrooms as a child were in direct opposition to what I saw and lived on a daily basis. To this day, I have a problem understanding how a pedophile could be a minister, professor and a community leader.

The result? Ignore religion. Ignore what I knew on an intellectual basis, and just live my life as I saw fit. So I achieved; did more and won more than my siblings. If I belonged to a group, then I'd be president of it; if I majored in theater, then I'd direct it. I eventually became a teacher and threw my whole self into it. I became Teacher of the Year.

I fell in love while teaching and spent three years in agony, while he was doing three tours in Vietnam. At the same time, my mother was dying with cancer. In October of 1969, she died. I felt then that I was free of keeping any appearance of a good relationship with the family for her sake. I just went my own way.

After his third tour, my boyfriend and I went to Canada for six months. He was AWOL from the army and I was AWOL from my family. After a while, that relationship fell apart, and I regained some sense and returned to Ole Miss and a Master's program. Of greatest importance, I also returned to my oldest sister, who lived on that campus. Through Pam's unconditional love and total acceptance, I was to form a bond with her that I have with nobody else. She has been the most powerful influence in my life, and she has been my lifeline through all I have done. All that is good, holy and Christ-like can be seen in her. Were it not for Pam, I would have lost contact with family. I abused her love so often – testing it time and time again and she has never wavered or let me down.

By age 36, I was a director of field operations, in charge of all franchise field operations for a large company. When a fiber optic cable was tested, I was the project team leader. I was national president of a technical organization, and regional president of our telecom association – the first female to hold either post. I was the only female member of Reagan's trade mission to Japan for telecom joint development. I was still trying to prove I could succeed – in spite of my father.

In 1987, the franchise division was sold off and finally disbanded. I had been sent to Houston, Texas, to try to salvage three central offices ravaged by the oil depression. I received a settlement, as a "buy-out' of contract from the company, and started my own company as a consultant. I blew a lot of the money. I tried to get the business off the ground but, because I was sick, I could not (or did not) have the drive and desire to see it through.

I came home, driven by the idea I would make peace with father and the family. That was the worst mistake, in a long line of them, that I ever made. At the age of 94, my father tried to abuse me again by getting in bed and displaying himself. Just the idea of his warped mind destroyed me again. His new wife came in as I was telling him to get out and what I thought of him, and she just hung her head and led him out.

I ran away again from everyone, and the base of it all was always my father. This time I really flipped. I was sentenced to 25 years for armed robbery, but 22 were suspended and I went to CMCF to complete the three mandatory years. I met the Chaplain and, next to my sister Pam, she became the major influence in my life. To be perfectly honest, if it had not been for Chaplain Hatcher, I would never have changed.

Once more I achieved— doing what I do best, running something! In prison there is a "pecking order" and I soon saw how that order went and set out to get to the top of the heap. It took six months to go from the kitchen (the lowest of the low), to working in the Identification Department, to the support clerk for the big boys (Director of accounting and the Superintendent). I had complete freedom of the compound and earned it with long hours and hard work, following 99 percent of the rules.

What I didn't see was how God was prodding me along His path, not mine. In my job I was put in daily contact with the Chaplain's Department. As a result, the friends I developed there were the women who were, for the most part, walking with Christ. I will always believe God put a huge stop sign in my own highway of life and said, *"Now, you've got to meet somebody you can trust, other than Sue, to live as a Christian."* See, I knew, from all those theology classes, how a Christian person should be. I had just never seen it outside of Pam and, heck, she was my sister. So I wasn't too sure how much was her love of me as her sister, or how much was from Christ-like behavior.

In Chaplain Hatcher, I finally had the living example of what I had been taught for years. And boy, did I test her and did I watch her, and did I question and did I ask, "*Is this lady real?*" I needed someone to show me that Christianity was real and not just a religious thing. By the Chaplain consistently displaying her belief, I could begin to believe. I still thank God daily that He brought me to her.

I spent every spare moment in the Chapel, surrounding myself with people I felt were changing their lives. Once again, the "take charge" took over, and I was constantly "doing" things for God and "His chapel."

My father died one August, and that morning was the first time I had verbalized what he and the family had done to me. I shared my story with the Chaplain. The release was so powerful. The opportunity just to say it was so astounding that I don't think I will ever forget it. I did not attend my father's funeral because the opportunity to do so was denied me, and very shortly afterward, I was released to parole status.

My father's estate was cleared, and I took that money and moved to a town near the prison, trying to surround myself with people who I knew would keep me strong and in the right path; failing to realize I was not strong and nobody could do that for me.

I was on five years probation and resented it so much. I loathed the state "system" and felt I had paid enough with the three years. I enjoyed the job I had, but I had not told them (on the advice of my parole officer) that I was a felon. An MDOC guard, moonlighting as their night security, caused me to lose the job.

I left the town again and struck out on my own with people I should never have been around. That led to going to Florida and being picked up, charged and brought back to Mississippi. My probation was revoked, and the 22-year sentence was given back to me. I found myself once again in CMCF. Once again God put a big "stop" sign in my life. I was isolated in Maximum Security for three months. In those months, I finally accepted what I had never really believed. I could spout Scripture and talk a wonderful talk, but I didn't accept it as Truth and believe it. I was as fake as my father was. I made the decision to stop being so smart about it all: to stop fixing, to stop doing, and to start living as Christ demands. To give up control. I finally understood where the peace and joy come from – and the only way to get it was to BELIEVE GOD IS IN CONTROL, no matter what. I realized He is not concerned about my abilities. He gave them to me. He is concerned about my availability to do it for Him, not those I admire; not anybody else, but Him. I stopped trying to become a Christian and just told God I will do whatever, wherever, but I had to know it was from Him – and not me.

For so long I thought I was a reprobate, put here for the purpose of showing people that not everyone can be saved. Mrs. Joyce Horton, a dear volunteer, got me past that, bless her soul.

I am at peace. I feel that no matter what happens, I am loved, protected and will be used for much good. For the first time in my life, I am content.

Ann was released from prison and became a dedicated member of her church, where her numerous creative gifts were much appreciated. She died after several years of freedom, and is sorely missed.

Cathy

I was raised in Pensacola, Florida, in a family that didn't have high moral values. My dad would hit my mother, so my brothers, sisters and I had to break them up from fighting. My dad was a flagrant man, and he would see other women. My big brother was my hero, but he wasn't the type of person I should have wanted to spend time with. He would smoke pot, run away from home, sneak out the window at night, and skip school during the day. Before long, I was doing those same things. I was sent to a detention home twice for running away. At an early age, I asked my parents if I could move out, for I thought they were too strict. Of course they said no.

When I was 16, I got pregnant, got married, and moved out anyway. It was John's amiable personality that attracted me to him, but he had been to prison once already and he was on the way back for violation of parole. He was sent away for two yeas. During this time, I was not a faithful wife waiting for my husband to return. No, I was just the opposite.

When John was released from prison, we started our life of crime together. We started burglarizing houses, dealing in drugs and then burglarizing drugstores. During these years, I started into the harder drugs. I would see our many friends come over to purchase the drugs we had available. To me, they were disgusting after shooting these drugs into their veins. I made a resolution that I would never stick a needle in my arm. Before long, however, I was doing exactly the same thing they were doing. The reason I began was because my husband started seeing other women. The first one stopped seeing him when I beat her up! I beat the second one up too, even going so far as sticking a gun to her head. She still kept seeing him, though, because he was supplying her with drugs. She liked getting the drugs from him more than she disliked getting beat up by me!

Eventually, we all moved in together. After months of seeing her get all this free dope from my husband, I got jealous because she was getting something from him that I wasn't. So, I began sticking a needle in my arm too. At first, it made me sick. My eyes were blurry, and I thought I was going to die. I was certain I wouldn't get hooked. I would see how she spent all her time messed up. If she didn't get the drugs, she would be sick and go through withdrawal symptoms. Still, I thought I could control the drugs. They wouldn't control me. But little did I know that it was Satan who planted that lie. If I hadn't turned a deaf ear to all that I heard about drugs, I wouldn't have gotten hooked. Someone should have hit me with a hammer to knock some sense into me. Once I had received the drugs into my system a number of times, I was hooked. I was helpless to even fight against it.

Because of drugs, I have faced death a number of times. I have overdosed several times. I have been shot, and I have been run over by a tractor. It is only by the grace of God and his mighty power that I am alive.

The police had been trying to catch us for some time, so we decided to move to Mississippi. Six months after we were there, we were arrested for possession of drugs. They tried to get information from me about others, but this little bird wasn't singing. I spent three days in jail, and then was released on bail. Those three days didn't teach me my lesson. I continued to do drugs.

A year later, I went to court and got 10 years. I was absolutely surprised. This was my first offense! I spent two months in jail, and then began reading my Bible and praying. I thought this was all there was to being a Christian. Volunteer Christians were not allowed to come to this jail. I had nobody to tell me that I needed a personal relationship with Jesus Christ. I was released on an appeal bond, put my Bible aside, quit praying and went back to doing drugs.

By this time, we were in deep financial trouble from paying so much to lawyers and bondsmen. We came back to Florida and were arrested again for possession. While I was in jail, I found that I was five months pregnant. I would have had an abortion if I could have. I had already had two abortions, because of the drugs I was doing. I thought surely something would be wrong with the babies. So I committed murder and got rid of them through abortion. At the time, I didn't see it as murder, but only as getting rid of my immediate problem. But it is murder. Since I couldn't get an abortion this time, I decided to bargain with God. I told him if I could get out, and if the baby would be born normal, I would quit drugs. I did get out, but I continued to do drugs. At 8 1/2 months, my little girl was born dead. After that, I went back to jail to wait for my court date.

Volunteer Christians came and shared the love of Jesus. This is when I saw that I needed Jesus Christ in my life, and accepted him as my personal Savior and Lord. Right away, He started making changes in my life. He helped me to stop smoking and cursing and, most important, he helped me with the inner changes that needed to be made. God's Word says, *"Though your sins be as scarlet, they shall be as white as snow. Though they be red like crimson, they shall be as wool."* So we all need Jesus. I was the happiest I had ever been in my life.

I was transferred to Mississippi to do my time for the crime I committed there. I fell when temptation came my way. I was no longer like a tree firmly planted. It was like someone had taken a saw and cut me down. After several months of turning away from Christ, I came back around and felt a strong desire to learn more about Jesus. He changed my life so much, and gave me a witness to share with others.

The chaplain invited me to work with her, and I was put on the chaplain's speaking team, where we went to the outside world to churches, to schools, to civic organizations wherever we were invited to share our testimony of what

Christ had done for us. What a privilege to be outside the prison, seeing the sights on our trips!

I was eventually released on bond after four years and 10 months in prison. I got a job the week I was released from prison. I got an apartment, and my son came to live with me. Many Christians helped me to get the things I needed, from butter to a broom. I was even allowed to go back into the prison as a volunteer chaplain. My Lord has blessed me so much that I want to shout to the world how much I love Him!

After settling into her freedom and a new life, Cathy was suddenly re-arrested and sent to Florida to serve time for a prior crime. I stayed in touch, and was gratified with her spiritual growth. After her release and a period of readjustment, Cathy met and married Cliff Pack. Cliff is in the remodeling business, and Cathy works as a secretary in a Florida church. They are both respected members of their community and church family.

Johnny

My family during childhood was dysfunctional due to having a mother and father who were alcoholics. By the time I was 5 years old, my two sisters, brother and myself were removed from my parents' custody. So began a life in the foster care system.

By the time I was 14, I had been in and out of approximately 25 to 30 foster homes. Some good, some bad, but mostly bad. Every home I found myself in, either the foster parent decided they didn't want me or else I didn't want them. I have been in homes where the foster parents were mentally, emotionally and physically abusive. Yes, to include sexually abusing helpless, hopeless children, male and female.

During my trips in and out of these foster homes, the caseworkers would periodically send me back to my biological parents, in hopes they had gotten their own lives together. On the surface, my parents would lead everyone to believe they had changed and were now wonderfully loving parents ready to take on the challenges of raising their children. It wouldn't be long before the caseworker would check up and remove us from their care and send me to yet another home.

I remember at roughly the age of 5, my Father would supply me with pints of 10-year-old charter whiskey, and would give it to me with the stipulation I had to start drinking and couldn't stop until I had finished off an entire pint of whiskey. Of course, being a young boy, I would do it thinking I was pleasing my Father.

My first sexual experience was at the age of 8. My parents left my sisters and myself with a 16-year-old female baby-sitter. After the baby sitter was able to get my sisters to go to sleep, she started having sexual intercourse with me. I wasn't old enough to understand what was going on, but now I know it would be called rape of a child.

Around 8 years old, I was allowed to start smoking cigarettes in my home. I had been caught many, many times sneaking around, stealing my parent's cigarettes. I would get into trouble for stealing them and that was it. My father and mother finally told me that when I could work and afford to buy my own, then I could smoke as openly as anyone else. Of course, the same day I was told this, I went to a service station, got a job, and came home that night with a carton of cigarettes.

By the age of 9, I was openly smoking marijuana with my friends, all of whom were teenagers. They were dope heads, so they had no problem with allowing and watching a 9-year-old get high and then laughing at me because I would be the clown of the bunch. I didn't care. I was getting high, and was fitting in with the older crowd. Around the age of 12, I graduated from marijuana to intravenously shooting up hard drugs. By the age of 14, I had quit school, and no one could tell me anything. Absolutely nothing! I was a young man who thought I knew it all. No one cared for me, and I neither loved or cared for anyone, except my Grandmother and myself.

I always worked, whether I was in a foster home or with my parents. I always liked having my own money because I could buy or fit into any crowd I wanted to hang out with. Of course, it was always the older crowd. At the age of 16, I got into trouble and my Grandmother had custody of me at that time. She was the one person in the world who constantly stayed in contact with me, wherever the system put me. I worshiped the ground she walked on because I believed she was the one person who actually cared about me. She was actually the only person I loved. When I got into trouble, she was given the choice of putting me in one of two state training schools. She convinced the court to allow her to pay and send me to French Camp, a Christian school for boys and girls. I entered French Camp and stayed there just long enough to get out from under the court order. Then I purposely got into trouble so that French Camp would kick me out. I started having different girls slip into my dormitory window, having sex with them and then sending them back out the same window. One night, a young lady was caught walking down the road after visiting me. The French Camp director asked her where she had been and she told him. Of course, I was immediately suspended. I didn't care. I just wanted out of that place.

I went back to my Grandmother's home. I was of an age when I didn't or wouldn't listen to anyone. So my Grandmother then sent me to live with Auntie and Uncle in Alabama and, believe me, I was a handful for anyone. About that time, my biological father died and I returned to Mississippi with a serious attitude. No one could control me. Life was nothing, except what Johnny wanted. My Grandmother convinced me to join the Job Corps. I started trouble there and was kicked out within two months.

I returned to living under my mother's roof with her live-in boyfriend. I would stay there from time to time, when I wasn't out running the streets. I could use alcohol, drugs and even bring girls to my Mother's house. I could do whatever I wanted under her roof, or go wherever I wanted. Still 16 years old, I remember my mother matchmaking me with an older woman (approximately 36-38). She was my Mother's friend, and I moved in with this older woman. She worked for a living and supplied me with drugs, alcohol and sex. I could do whatever I wanted during the day, but at night I belonged to her. Also, my sister had other friends of hers who liked me, or thought I was cute, and my sister would make deals for drugs in exchange for the sex I provided to her older girlfriends. Yes, my sister was very much into drugs, alcohol and sex. She was raped at the very early age of 7 or 8 by one of my mother's boyfriends and was sexually abused in at least one of the foster homes we stayed in.

By the age of 17, I was selling more drugs and making more money in a week than some people make in a year. I was seeking nothing except what pleased Johnny. I had plenty of money and drugs, constantly with different women, and I drove the fastest cars. I believed I was living the good life.

Then my life actually went from bad to worse. I moved to another town, where I managed to meet a cousin of mine I had never known before. I knew he was an outlaw who had been in and out of prison, living the same lifestyle as I was. Due to my lack of family growing up, I was never taught morals, values or anything else of that nature. Now I met this cousin who was older than me, and I had myself a role model. He was a major drug dealer who got shipments of drugs in from all over the United States. At first, I was just making small drug deals for him, yet my income increased many-fold. He then graduated me from small time drug dealer to a "pack mule." He would provide the vehicle and money and would send me west, and I would go to make major drug pick-ups for him. I'd then bring the drugs back into

Mississippi, where he would in turn distribute them. Sometimes everything ran smoothly and other times it didn't. But I always made sure to get away and return to Mississippi with the drugs.

It wasn't too many trips before he started running into competition in relation to the drugs. He was being undercut with the price, so the supplier changed hands. He knew who the competition was and decided to start allowing them to bring the dope into Mississippi. Then he would send two or three armed individuals who would rob the drug dealer bringing in the shipment of drugs. I participated in one of the armed robberies where we went in and took the cash and drugs from some other men. I really saw nothing wrong with it. I figured he was a drug dealer, so no one would care. Besides, I knew this cousin had several individuals working for him and they were into all kinds of crimes. while I was just a small fish in a large pond.

A couple of the guys who worked for this cousin were arrested. They were all ex-felons. They were very bad men, but convinced certain officials they were not the bad guys...I was! They did, in fact, tell the truth about my participation in robbing one individual, but they also told numerous lies. Needless to say, my being a teenager, when I was arrested I wasn't willing to cooperate with the law officers. I had been brainwashed by this cousin into believing that, no matter what, you do not tell on your buddies in crime. This was my hero telling me these things and I believed any and everything he said. He told me to keep my mouth shut about everything, and he would have me out of jail in no time. He explained that no matter what they questioned me about, I knew nothing. I did exactly what he said, and I was charged with two counts of armed robbery. He had me out on bail shortly after. While in jail, I was questioned about crimes I knew about and other crimes I knew nothing about. Some I was involved with, but others I wasn't. However, I maintained that I knew nothing about any of it. Some of these law officers actually told me they knew I wasn't involved in some of the crimes, but if I didn't cooperate, they were going to charge me with so many crimes I would never see the light of day again.

I ended up being convicted of two counts of armed robbery and given a life-plus-20-year sentence. I did, in fact, participate in one of the robberies, but was totally innocent of the other. I was the fall guy for all of my so-called friends.

After being in Parchman, I came to find out that not only was I the fall guy, but I had been set up. The cousin, of whom I thought so highly, had set me up from day one. I was the youngest of his group of outlaws, and he knew I wasn't going to implicate him or any of his co-conspirators. I would be the one sent down the river without a paddle! This cousin made all sorts of promises that he would have me out in approximately three to five years, and to remain keeping my mouth shut because if he or any of his buddies were caught, they would be sentenced to life without parole because they were ex-felons. I remained incarcerated for more than 20 years.

Before I went to Parchman, I convinced a friend of mine, who was pregnant with my daughter, to marry me. I didn't marry her because I loved her; I married her because my grandmother told me it was the right thing to do, considering she was pregnant with my child. Besides, the girl had been living with me on and off for approximately five years and I needed her companionship while in prison and also to smuggle drugs, money and such into the prison. I was first locked up in 1983, and this marriage lasted a couple of years.

While in Parchman, I continued to sell and use drugs. I would have visitors bring me drugs, but most of the drugs came from officers within the system, who I would pay off to supply them. I had several officers who would bring whatever I requested.

At this time, my life was still only about what Johnny wanted, but deep in my heart and soul, I had never found peace. Even while in prison, I still had different females coming to see me and still had plenty of drugs and money, but something was missing and, no matter how I searched, I couldn't find what I was looking for.

I was working a gymnasium job in the prison system, and the Chaplain's Department was located in the gym. There was a chaplain who knew I was into all sorts of illegal activities while in prison, but he saw something in me I never knew was there. He always tried to make conversation. Being polite, I would allow him to speak, but was waiting for him to start preaching and then I was going to verbally assault him. He never did! Instead he asked me to start taking pictures on visitation day for the Chaplain's Department. Of course, I agreed because that would be a way for me to further my illegal activities.

For several months I worked part-time for this Chaplain, and one day as he was leaving, he handed me a Bible and walked away. Said nothing, just handed me a Bible! I started to throw it in the trash, but didn't. Instead I carried it back to my cell, threw it in my locker and didn't think any more about it. Just before Christmas one year, I was feeling alone and depressed, wondering if I was ever going to get out of prison. I looked into my locker and that Bible was just reaching out to me. I picked it up and opened to the inscription on the front cover, which quoted Psalm 119:11. At first I paid no attention to that Scripture; I just started reading bits and pieces of the Bible. I was lonely, bored, with nothing to do, so why not read some of it? I had to make sure none of the other convicts saw me reading the Bible because that was for weak individuals who needed a crutch in life.

Anyway, I found myself reading stories in the Bible, and then I decided to check out the Scripture the Chaplain had listed. I looked up Psalm 119:11 and it said, *"Thy Word have I hid in my heart that I may not sin against thee."* I immediately burst into tears and cried better than a 3-year-old child. It seemed the tears would never stop flowing, and I accepted Christ into my life at that very moment. No one was around; it was just God and me in that little ole cell. I continued to read the Bible, but I wouldn't openly discuss what had happened, nor would I allow anyone to see me reading the Bible. I was still full of pride and thought I had an image as a hard-core convict to uphold. I was still into some illegal activity, but slowly I found my bad habit of drug use slowed down – and then stopped. I didn't want to use drugs anymore. I was still selling drugs and making money for survival in the system, but even that started slowing down, and I would only sell enough to get me by.

It seemed like the more I got away from illegal activities, the better my life was getting, and I was feeling much better about myself as a person. I eventually was transferred from Parchman to Central Mississippi Correctional Facility. By this time, my greatest sins were anger, pride, envy and such. I had gotten completely away from using or selling drugs.

After arriving at CMCF, I was put to work for the Fire Department there, and I met another Chaplain, Wendy "Ma" Hatcher, who took an interest in me. I began working part-time for the Chaplains' Department there, too. This time I was a young, immature Christian, who was growing and seeking to do good things in life. I found my life was being blessed in so many ways, but I still struggled to show love or express love to anyone. I knew God loved me and expected me to love others. The only person to whom I showed love was my Grandmother. I still didn't trust people enough to express love to them.

Then my world was turned upside down. My Grandmother died, and it broke my heart. The only people I ever cared for were my father, brother and grandmother. Now all three were dead and, from an earthly aspect, I was all alone. Chaplain Hatcher knew I was hurting, and she stepped in to show me there were other people who cared about me. I finally did learn to love others, but I struggled with allowing them to love me. I think I was afraid I would be hurt again.

Chaplain Hatcher believed I had a story that needed to be shared with others. She had me speak to groups within the prison and would carry me to different places outside the prison, as part of the "Captives for Christ" speaking team, in hope it would influence others to come to know God and help assist them in making the right choices in life. We also wanted to show people that prisoners too can come to know God and allow Him to change their lives.

I was involved in every church activity CMCF had to offer. I helped build a new chapel building in order to accommodate the rapidly growing prison population. My life was blessed in so many ways. For example, even though incarcerated, the officials allowed me to do certain things within the prison that helped me to grow spiritually. Every Christmas and Easter a group of fellow convicts would get together, under the Chaplain's supervision, to put on skits and plays for the entire population and staff members. We did have a lot of fun, but we considered it a way to serve our Lord.

I was allowed to attend and train at the Mississippi State Fire Academy, where I received as much training as any fireman in the United States. Prison personnel would actually release me at the Fire Academy each morning. Then, when I finished training that evening, I would call the prison and they would pick me up.

I met a very special female convict and, over a 3-year span, I grew to mentally, emotionally and spiritually worship the ground she walked on. Three years later, I asked this beautiful, wonderful, God-fearing woman to marry me. She agreed to become my wife, but the prison wouldn't allow it. It wasn't until three years later and submitting applications each year, that permission was finally granted.

I became eligible for parole in 1993 and went before the parole board, highly recommended by prison staff, seven times. For almost 20 years, my prison record was impeccable and I accomplished so much. I have been forgiven for my ugly past by a God who knows my heart. I have to admit I didn't understand why I wasn't released earlier, but I have come to understand that *"all things work together for those who love God and are called according to His purpose."* (Phil 4:28 KJV).

According to God's Word, He has taught me there are three types of love. One is God's love, another is the love for friends and family, and the third is the love for a spouse. I have grown to understand, accept and apply all three to my life. God, Wendy Hatcher, volunteer Chaplain Ben Malone and Wanda Rutland Thrasher, have taught me all three, and for that I will always be grateful. I am blessed with a wonderful wife, friends, family and an eternal salvation that only God can supply.

Chaplain's Note: Because of a lawsuit through the federal courts, where it was ruled that marriage is a right and not a privilege, convicts were allowed to marry, including fellow convicts. Requests for this "right" were numerous. I was opposed to convict marriages partially because I believed that most prisoners married only to take advantage of Mississippi's long-time conjugal visitation program, which was intended to keep families together in spite of incarceration. However, I was primarily concerned because I saw the additional heartache it often brought to the married couples. I remember saying to Superintendent Roberts, "the divorce rate will be incredible," to which he replied, "it's that way in society as well." He was right, of course.

Johnny's request to marry a lovely, Christian female convict was denied three times before they received reluctant permission. I suppose because I knew both Johnny and Wanda so well, I felt theirs would be a marriage to strengthen them both in their faith. After the ceremony, Johnny was immediately transferred to Parchman, in spite of the fact that other married convict couples remained in the same prison with the privilege of every Sunday visitation.

Johnny brought a discrimination suit against the MDOC and, after three years, was returned to CMCF. During those three difficult years, Johnny and Wanda kept their marriage alive through the mail, and both matured spiritually. Both Johnny and Wanda have been paroled for years now, and their marriage remains strong after 17 years.

Stu

My childhood was anything but normal. I was raised in staff residences on the grounds of Mississippi State Penitentiary (Parchman) and though I had caring, good parents, I felt alone and scared.

My mother was Administrator for the women at the prison. The lady inmates would take care of me after school and also when my parents were at work. They also taught me how to pick door locks and cheat pretty well at cards. I rode horses with some of the men. A few of them became like a father and a brother to me. I would idolize them. They made me feel important and wanted. One day, a horrible nightmare happened to me. I was out riding bikes with another employee's son. He said he wanted to ride to the dairy unit on the compound to buy some snacks from the canteen. While we were inside, the inmate clerk came from behind the counter and locked the door. Though I was young, I knew something was terribly wrong. The inmate grabbed me from behind and violently raped me, while my friend watched the door. My "friend" set me up. After some time, the man threatened my life, but he let me go. I rode home in pain alone, very alone. I never told anyone about this life-changing incident until I was 30 years old in a treatment center for compulsive gambling.

Not long after this occurred, I heard for the first time in my life that God's son died on the cross for my sins and that I could have peace and joy. That's what I needed. Though I didn't respond, I listened.

My parents, who had tried everything from psychologists to hospital care, finally sent me to a Christian boarding school. Only two months after arriving, I gave my life to Jesus Christ. However, I never grew in the Lord; I never had a consistent walk, and was never lead by the Spirit. I figured out what to say and when to say it. I had a "form of Godliness but no power." I just became an actor, a very good actor at times.

I eventually graduated from high school as a popular "Christian" leader. I attended college and met the lady I would eventually marry – a beautiful Christian woman. After a very romantic courtship, we married in a fairy tale wedding.

We bought a large beautiful home. We had great jobs, great friends and were planning a family. We were perceived to have it all together. I was considered a godly man and husband.

Three days before our first anniversary, I made a decision that would change the course of our lives forever. I started gambling in Mississippi's numerous casinos. I chose to walk away from everything God, in His Grace, had given me, but most of all to walk away from Him.

My life eventually turned to crime to support my addictions to gambling. Then from crime to probation, from probation to prison, with a 27-year sentence for forgery and bad checks. I thought I had come to the end of my rope; 27 years to serve, destruction of a wonderful marriage, and the shame of having to leave the ministry and destroy what witness I had for Christ.

A miracle occurred when, through the interception of influential Christian friends, the Governor of Mississippi granted me clemency when he retired from office. I thought I had "whipped" this gambling addiction, but that was my problem. I had done nothing. I had only arrested the problem – which was to be expected since there are no casinos in prison. I thought by abstaining from something that I was cured. Because I didn't face much temptation, I thought I could resist it when I was released.

I was not walking in the Spirit. I was doing everything in my own power, my own strength, my own will. Needless to say, I failed. I violated executive clemency and violated a 27-year suspended sentence that I had received.

I should be dead, by all rights. God should have taken my life but instead, by His mercy and only by His Grace, I am back in prison. Also, only by His Grace, my mind is back and my heart has yielded and returned to Him. I have learned the hard way to humble myself before the Lord and to be content to live my life in prison.

When Stu was still serving his sentence in a county satellite prison, he wrote to me: "My destructive life has put understandable wedges between myself and many people. I have racked my brain trying to understand why I became what I am. How could I do the things I did? All I know is that sin is destructive. And sin is addictive. There is no excuse, for we are all without excuse, especially one such as I who have been given so much. I am humbled by the destruction my sin Has caused. I haven't wanted to face many people since my arrest; the young people I had witnessed to; the ones I led to Christ…why He is still merciful, I don't understand. I know it is my fault. No one, absolutely no one is to blame but myself."

Pauline

I was born in a small rural town on the Mississippi Gulf Coast, the eldest of eleven siblings in very impoverished conditions. My dad worked all the time, (pulp wood business owner) and so did my Mom. We used outside toilets and hauled water from the creek, using broom handles and buckets. My dad was killed at the hands of my mother as I witnessed. I helped her lift him and put him in the car to get him to the hospital. My Grandmother and my Mother's baby sister kept us ninety-nine percent of the time.

Grandmother was a devout Christian and Sunday school teacher and very much the strength of our family. She was quite strict, but she brought joy to us all. She cooked, crocheted, quilted and read the Bible continuously. She didn't believe in idleness, as she felt this gave place for getting into trouble, and she was very active in the Church. Every first and third Sundays we were committed to prepare meals for the Pastor and all of his guests. We were so poor we didn't have air conditioning, but my grandmother had a solution! She would take cardboard boxes and reinforce then with electrical tape to make them sturdy enough for us to use as fans. While the preacher and his family and guests ate, we were required to fan them until they departed from the table. To my grandmother, it was a form of honoring leadership. After the meal we would clean the kitchen and then Grandmother would go over her next Sunday school lesson and teach it to us. The following Sunday she would review it again with us, Expecting us to answer questions.

My nickname was "Cinderella" because all I did was work and care for younger siblings. I was, and remain, oversized. That added to my determination to be the "royal" one in the family—the princess, or the queen. I always dreamed BIG. I was going to be rich and rescue all of my family from the curse and shame of poverty. I told myself this hundreds of times. *"Pauline, you are the One."*

In order to help care for and feed my ten siblings, I would dress them and go to every funeral no matter the ethnicity of the deceased, just for the opportunity to attend the repast to feed my siblings. This went on for years until one sibling was crying profusely at the funeral. She looks at me with those red teary eyes and asked, "What relative or friend is this," for the first time. I simply had run out of answers and felt, my "cover was blown." I was "busted" and I need other options to help my family.

After I left home I would always read my Bible, but there were those in my new circle who told me that would only drive me crazy, so I became confused and rebellious. I was suffering from identity crisis.

I began doing wrong. It was common for me to steal from local stores. When I finished high school and started my year of college, I opened my first checking account and my first credit card. I did well for a while and thought I had arrived. Well. After the money was gone, I continued to write checks. The bank paid the first check and I continued writing checks on an account with insufficient funds. This landed me in the county jail. Some family members and friends paid the fine and I was released. I was never booked, never fingerprinted, nor was a mug shot taken, and I didn't see the inside of the jail. I did not learn a lesson. I continued to write bad checks, again and again.

About this time I met a preacher who was teaching the "prosperity" message and I thought, "yes, this is just where I am." I was certainly looking the part, because, "things" had become very important to me. In my mind this is what made the rich and famous. The prosperity message is what I wanted to hear, and this preacher assured me that God intends for Christians to have everything they want. My life of crime escalated because it wasn't just for me. I had siblings who were dependent upon me as well, and I tried to get them everything they needed and wanted to overcome the shame and embarrassment they felt in school.

My crime spree got worse and worse and spread statewide, landing me in the county jail. This time there was fingerprinting, mug shots and I was taken to a cell. There was no bail and a court date was set. I stayed in the county jail for one year prior to going to court and was sentenced to six years in the Mississippi Department of Corrections. Reality hit me!

Before being transferred, there were volunteers (Christians) coming to the jail sharing the message and love of Jesus. I would just slam my door because I had been in church all my life and I thought I knew all there was to know about Jesus. I did not want to hear their message. Week after week they came back, knowing I would close the door. Then

I began leaving a crack in the door, and finally one day, in a broken state, I committed my life and surrendered my all into the hands of Jesus. I haven't been the same since. This did not change my sentence, but I experienced a peace I had never known.

After getting to the prison, I participated in the religious programs and church services, where I met Chaplain Hatcher. She selected me from hundreds of women she had chosen to work for her. I knew then about the favor of God. The chaplain whom I call "Maw" nurtured me in the Word and discipled me, and shared her heart and love with me. I felt like a little girl all over again. She nurtured me in a way that a mother would nurture a baby.

Going to the prison was the best thing that ever happened to me...because I found Jesus.

Pauline has been out of prison for more than 25 years now. She is married to Freddie (whose testimony also appears here), was a highly esteemed medical assistant for 25 years, and is currently the Missions and Outreach Director of her local Church, and the Co-founder of the Reaching and Educating for Community Hope (RECH) Foundation. In May 2015, Pauline was appointed the Field Director for Prison Fellowship for the state of Mississippi. Prison Fellowship is the nation's largest outreach to prisoners, ex-prisoners and their families, founded by White House former Nixon aide, Chuck Colson. In 2012, Pauline followed the calling of God to start the "Wendy Hatcher Transitional House" for female ex-offenders, and is currently raising the funds to purchase the home in Jackson and launch the ministry. I feel greatly honored to have such a devoted friend and to have my name on a home that will continue to nurture those in need long after I am gone from this earth.

Freddie

On April 21, 1976, I left home "joy riding" with a few of my friends. It took me 15 years, 8 months and 22 days before I returned home. That night we did an armed robbery for which I was sentenced, at the age of 15, to serve 30 years in the Mississippi Department of Corrections.

I entered Parchman, not really knowing what to expect. I found a jungle in which I had no other choice but to become a part, unless I wanted to be eaten alive. I, too, became a beast in order to survive.

After my arrival, other convicts began to tutor me in how to make it in "their world," which was totally different from the world from which I was taken. In 1979, I stabbed another convict. It was by God's Grace he didn't die (although I didn't see it that way at the time). I received an additional 15 years for assault and attempted murder. Now my sentence became 45 years. Then I got involved in a scheme with money orders, before that eventually got me another 20 years. My whole life flashed before me. I had placed myself in a position for now serving a whopping 65 years, and it seemed to me at that time it would be very, very unlikely that I would ever see or taste freedom again.

I was transferred to Central Mississippi Correctional Facility. I soon thought I had discovered where "the action" was…in the chaplains' department. I told the chaplain later that I watched convicts coming from her office grinning and I thought, *"that must be where the dope is."* I found out later that it was another kind of "high."

The day I realized that I was just "tired of being tired," I made a request to see the chaplain. It had been over 12 years since I knew what it felt like to cry. Even when I lost my father, my heart was so hard I couldn't make myself cry, because I thought that was a sign of weakness. On this day, sitting in the chaplain's office, I was touched by God and I began to cry uncontrollably. It seemed as though a dam had been broken. After all those years, I realized that God created man, therefore God has the power to change a man's heart. Man couldn't do it. Even the System, where people have placed their faith in rehabilitation, couldn't do it. Jesus accepted me just the way I was, messed up and full of sin. I have been walking with Him ever since, far from perfectly, but determinedly.

After I miraculously received parole, God gave me a wife who loves God more than she loves me. People said our marriage wouldn't last a year because we are both ex-cons, but we have been married now for 21 years. I have learned, and am still learning, that God, not people, makes the difference.

Since my release in November of 1991, I've been involved in prison ministry, for the simple reason that Christ loved me when I was unlovable. I am reminded about Jonah from the Bible. At one time, we all ran from God and disobeyed that voice. God has shown me that storms are a part of the Christian life and sometimes we have that "whale" experience. It is in those times of being "in the belly" that God is shaping us into the people that He would have us to be.

Freddie has been out of prison for 23 years and is now an ordained minister, with a true servant's heart. He recently said, *"May God continue to use people in all walks of life to reach others for His Kingdom. I pray that we, as soldiers of the Lord, will always look at people with the Lord's eyes and not our own. Love is what love does*!

Joe

I grew up on the south-side of Chicago. There were 11 children, and I am the youngest. At the age of 10, I made a decision to be like two of my older brothers; the oldest was a gangster and the youngest was a pickpocket. They both impressed me because they never worked, but had all the material trappings. When I was 11 years old, the gangster was killed, found dead on the west side of Chicago. He was shot in the head, and found behind a dumpster. Although one of my idols, his death was not enough to cause me not to pursue that lifestyle.

By the time I was 13, stealing, drinking, smoking and drugs were an everyday thing. When I was 16, my brother who picked pockets turned me out, meaning that he taught me to pick pockets. That is what I did for the next couple of years. I also found myself going to jail quite often.

After my second trip to Cook County Jail, I was shipped to Mississippi by my older siblings. That is where my parents are from, and they had moved back after my brother, Tommy, was killed. When I moved to Mississippi, my activities of crime did not stop. The type of crime I was committing just changed. I found myself in Parchman prison as a young man 18 years of age.

I was released shortly before my 21st birthday. I was out of prison about two months, and the brother who trained me to pick pockets was stabbed 23 times and killed. After six months, I found myself arrested again for robbing a drug house. I received a 20 year mandatory sentence. While in the R&D center in Parchman, I began to take stock of my life, which was shaping up to be just like my brothers…from drug addiction, in and out of prison, and all the heartaches and pains. I knew then, if I continued to live that type of lifestyle, I would end up dead at an early age. My first brother was killed when he was 21. The second brother was 29 at the time of his death. I knew that was my fate.

Literally shaken by the thought of ending up dead before I was 30, the Holy Spirit began to deal with me. I went down on my knees, repented of all the wrong I had done, and asked Christ to show me what it meant to believe in Him. And Christ did just that. He brought people into my life that discipled me in the grace of God. I am so grateful for people like Odell Fish and "Ma" Wendy Hatcher. The Lord was gracious to me again in 1988, when the governor of Mississippi granted me clemency. I was released 10 years and 4 months early.

I knew God had called me to the gospel ministry. After being released from prison, I attended Belhaven University for my undergrad degree and from there, I went to Reformed Theological Seminary. I now pastor a small Presbyterian Church of America in Tallahassee, Florida. To God Be The Glory.

CPSIA information can be obtained
at www.ICGtesting.com
Printed in the USA
LVOW04s1238090616

491676LV00002BA/2/P